# HEALTHY DIVORCE

# Healthy
# Divorce

CRAIG EVERETT, Ph.D.

SANDRA VOLGY EVERETT, Ph.D.

JOSSEY-BASS PUBLISHERS · SAN FRANCISCO

FIRST PAPERBACK EDITION PUBLISHED IN 1998

Jossey-Bass books and products are available through most bookstores. To contact Jossey-Bass directly, call (888) 378-2537, fax to (800) 605-2665, or visit our website at www.josseybass.com.

Substantial discounts on bulk quantities of Jossey-Bass books are available to corporations, professional associations, and other organizations. For details and discount information, contact the special sales department at Jossey-Bass Inc., Publishers.

TCF Manufactured in the United States of America on Lyons Falls Turin Book. This paper is acid-free and 100 percent totally chlorine-free.

Library of Congress Cataloging-in-Publication Data

Everett, Craig A.
Healthy divorce / Craig A. Everett and Sandra Volgy Everett. —1st ed.
p.   cm.—
Includes bibliographical references (p.   ) and index.
ISBN 0-7879-4381-9 (paperback)
ISBN 1-55542-672-7 (hardcover)
I. Divorce—United States—Psychological aspects. I. Everett, Sandra Volgy II. Title. III. Series.
HQ834. E94 1994
306.89—dc20                                                                                        94-12541

FIRST EDITION
HB Printing
10  9  8  7  6  5  4  3  2  1

PB Printing
10  9  8  7  6  5  4  3  2

# Contents

# Acknowledgments

OUR DEFINITION OF THE STAGES of divorce has been evolving since we worked together at the Pima County Conciliation Court in Arizona in the early 1980s. In 1987 we began conducting workshops for other professionals on working with divorcing families. The stages that we describe in this book were first introduced to other therapists in a chapter we wrote for *The Handbook of Family Therapy*, Volume II (1991), edited by Alan Gurman and David Kniskern.

Many colleagues have been influential in our work. But we would like particularly to acknowledge three individuals: Judge Norman Fenton for his support in our early work in divorce at the Conciliation Court in Tucson; our friend and attorney, Gary Grynkewich, who has reviewed and made suggestions on our discussions of legal aspects of divorce; and our friend and colleague, Dan Kiley, whose enthusiasm and helpful suggestions kept us motivated. We have valued the assistance of our editor, Alan Rinzler, and the energy and tireless work of our secretary, Mrs. Elizabeth Schlecter, who has prepared several versions of this manuscript.

Most of all we wish to acknowledge the many couples and families with whom we have been privileged to work. We have learned much from their struggles and accomplishments. We hope their efforts will be something of a legacy in helping you to achieve a Healthy Divorce!

# Introduction

IVORCE IS ONE OF THE MOST CONFUSING and disturbing events most people ever experience. It disrupts their relationships, their sense of continuity in life, the very core of their identity.

Many books offer advice about "surviving" divorce—how to handle it legally and emotionally, how to help your children survive the experience. We believe, however, that there are ways to approach divorce in a more positive manner, a way that helps you do better than just survive. We think that you can actually have what we call a "healthy divorce." In a healthy divorce, a constructive rather than destructive transition out of marriage is planned and accomplished, and both parents and children return to normal, happy functioning as rapidly as possible.

To accomplish this goal requires both an informed understanding of the divorce process and the willingness to undertake specific tasks and work toward specific goals. For the sake of your own adjustment and the well-being of your children, you need to learn how to approach divorce constructively. We're convinced that by knowing what to expect in the divorce process, and understanding the varied emotions that are present in the family throughout the experience, you can minimize the pain and disruption.

In this book we describe predictable stages of divorce—from the earliest unsettled feelings of dissatisfaction to planning a separation, dealing with legal issues, remarrying, and forming a new, blended

1

family. Throughout these stages we identify specific goals and tasks to help make the experience healthier. We also provide numerous examples of how other divorcing families have handled their experiences in both healthy and unhealthy ways.

Divorce is a continuum of stages, each one typically bound to and emerging from the stage before. In a healthy divorce there are three overall tasks:

1. Letting go

2. Developing new social ties

3. Redefining parental roles

By recognizing these stages in the divorce process you can build a faith that "this too shall pass" and that along the way there are tasks to be accomplished that may turn the tide of events in your favor. This does not mean you will avoid pain and anger. But you and your children will benefit from a greater understanding of the feelings and events that go with divorce, a very significant life transition for everyone involved.

We are a husband-and-wife team of therapists. Sandy is a clinical child psychologist who specializes in work with children and families. Craig is a marriage and family therapist working with a variety of family dysfunctions. He has also edited the *Journal of Divorce and Remarriage* for over ten years. We combine about forty-five years of experience, more than half that time specializing in families of divorce, first in the court and legal setting and later in academic and private settings. We have encountered a broad variety of experiences with families struggling to survive and rebuild through the divorce process.

For a number of years we directed programs for the Superior Court of Pima County in Tucson, Arizona. During that period, we tried to educate judges and attorneys about the special needs of parents who must enter the court system to secure their divorce. We conducted more than five hundred custody evaluations for the court, where we had to make recommendations about which parent should have custody, what type of custody and what kind of access plan would best serve the emotional and developmental needs of the children. We also developed mediation services for divorcing parents—more humane ways of helping families make responsible and reasonable decisions about their postdivorce needs and the living arrangements for their children.

*Healthy Divorce* is written for people who are considering the possibility of a divorce, presently going through the divorce process, or already divorced and working to redefine their life or a new family system. If you are considering a divorce, the goals and stages we present can help you know what to expect and perhaps identify windows of opportunity for trying to repair the difficulties in the marriage. If you are in the middle of the divorce process, our discussions will help you understand the issues and emotions that you and your children are dealing with and help you develop some goals to make the experience healthier. If you have been divorced recently (in the past few years), this book can help you look back and resolve some of the conflicts you endured and help you identify healthy goals for yourself and your children in the crucial postdivorce adjustment period.

Much of the focus of this book will be on divorcing families with children. If you do not have children or your children are grown, the early chapters about making the decision to divorce and letting go emotionally will probably be most relevant. And if you are considering remarrying someone who has children, the latter chapters on issues of blended families and stepparenting will be of interest.

In our work with couples, we view the divorce experience as occurring within each individual's broader family system. All people are a part of their own current nuclear family as well as an intergenerational system that defines their loyalties and ties to parents, siblings, and grandparents.

When a major event like divorce occurs in one part of this system, it creates shock waves. The entire system becomes unbalanced. Therefore it's important to understand the experience of divorce not just for yourself but as it affects and will be influenced by many other members of your family system. Your divorce may hurt them deeply. On the other hand, they can help you. Siblings, parents and grandparents can offer significant emotional and financial resources as you go through the divorce.

*Healthy Divorce* describes a concrete, practical process we have learned from the families we have worked with over the years. We will try to be specific and practical. It's also important to note that we have both been through the divorce process ourselves. So we know that what you need are clear, straightforward guidelines that can help you understand the complicated maze you're traveling through, and also offer some hope and direction for you and your children.

In the first chapter we offer our understanding of four main principles of the divorce experience. These are aspects of the divorce process that everyone experiences and should understand from the outset.

The core of the book—chapters Two through Nine—defines the fourteen stages of the divorce process. We share with you some of the struggles and challenges our clients have experienced, in the hope that they will serve as red-flag warnings of potential pitfalls.

We then take another look at the couple whose story opens the book, and conclude with answers to the most common questions about divorce. At the end of the book we include several resources that we believe can be helpful to you: a reading list of other books about divorce for parents and children (Appendix A); a list of professional organizations that you can contact for further help (Appendix B); and a model divorce agreement (Appendix C).

Now let's preview the actual stages of the divorce process:

## The 14 Stages of Divorce

1. *The clouds of doubt:* early warning signs in the gradual erosion of the marriage.

2. *The cold shoulder:* a variety of distancing behaviors caused by dissatisfaction in the marriage.

3. *Preseparation fantasies:* the emotional experience of imagining living without your spouse or substituting new partners and lovers.

4. *The showdown—physical separation:* the drama of planning to separate physically and preparing the children for the experience.

5. *Pseudoreconciliation:* struggles with loneliness, guilt, and the concerns for the children that lead to second thoughts about separation.

6. *Predivorce fantasies:* when efforts at reconciliation have failed and you begin to plan more earnestly for divorce rather than separation.

7. *The decision to divorce:* the final turning point, when both spouses and the children must come to grips with the ending of the marriage.

8. *Ambivalence:* the complexity and magnitude of the actual legal process trigger more second thoughts about whether you are making the right decision.

9. *Mediation:* a reasonable and peaceful method for ending a marriage without becoming enemies or dragging the children into an adversarial legal battle.

10. *The adversarial divorce:* the court battle that must occur if attempts at reasonable agreements fail.

11. *Co-parenting after the divorce:* developing new boundaries and roles as single yet cooperating parents and providing stability for your children.

12. *The first remarriage:* preparing both the children and the former spouse for the entrance of a new parent into the family system.

13. *The second remarriage:* pressures on the unmarried parent to create a new family system and restore the balance between the two families.

14. *A blended family:* structuring a healthy stepfamily that provides stability and satisfaction for you and your children; the final phase of the divorce process.

All these principles, stages, and goals are based on the issues we work on every day in our practices. Working with our clients, we have observed and learned the kinds of tasks that can improve the divorce experience. We are optimistic that parents and children can get through a divorce in a healthy and constructive manner and go on to enjoy their lives. From our own experience and from those of hundreds of our clients we can happily report that yes, there really is life after divorce!

# 1

# Understanding the Divorce Experience

I MET HER IN THE WAITING ROOM and knew immediately that she was struggling with a difficult crisis. Her hair was dull, her eyes puffy and red, her clothes somber. It appeared that she hadn't slept well in quite some time. With glazed eyes and a beaten-down appearance, she followed me into my office, unsure of where to sit or what to do. I pointed to a chair.

She sat down and started to cry. Slowly, the story came. Her husband had announced two nights before that he didn't love her any more and planned to move out and file for divorce. She had asked if there was another woman but he hadn't answered. He had simply said he had thought about this for a long time and he was sorry but he couldn't keep living a lie when he had no love left for her.

She was scared, confused, and angry. She hadn't told the kids yet. He told her to wait until he was ready to tell them but she knew they could tell already that something was terribly wrong. They kept asking what was going on, why their parents weren't speaking to each other, and why she kept running to her bedroom in tears. She didn't know what to tell them or how to tell them. She didn't know how to tell her friends and family. She didn't know how she was going to live through the awful pain and shock.

Janet knew that the marriage had had a certain emptiness for a long time. Communication was limited to things about the kids. Sex had been less and less frequent, and they never did much together as a couple any more. But she believed Jim loved his family and that their marriage was pretty much like everyone else's they knew: he was busy building his insurance business and she was busy raising the kids and working part-time.

They had been married thirteen years. Their oldest child was twelve, their youngest was six, and the middle child just turned ten; all the children were doing pretty well. She had thought their life was settled and stable. She had felt fortunate. Now she wondered how she could have been so dumb. How could she have ignored all the signs? She desperately wished she could change his mind and make this nightmare go away. She was willing to do anything.

On the other hand, her best friend (the only person she had told) said she should go get the meanest attorney she could find, take all the money out of their joint accounts, begin legal proceedings so she would have the upper hand, and show him what life could be like if he left her. This friend advised her to file for sole custody, spousal maintenance, and child support and make sure he got all the debts. Her own divorce five years earlier had been really dirty and she felt she had been taken advantage of by being too easy.

I asked Janet if she thought Jim might come talk to me; she said she'd ask him but she wasn't optimistic. I asked her not to do anything legally until we could sort out what was happening and decide on the best choices.

Jim did agree to come in. He arrived looking cautious and somewhat defensive, dressed neatly in a conservative business suit. He explained that for several years he had been trying to get Janet to recognize that their marriage was in trouble but she would get so emotional and defensive that he just stopped trying. He felt trapped in a marriage without love or sex and finally decided he didn't want to live the rest of his life feeling that way. He had become attracted to a lady at work several months ago and they had become sexually involved. He didn't want to hurt his wife or kids but he felt he was fighting for his life and had finally gotten the courage to tell her it was over.

Jim felt terribly guilty and wanted to help Janet any way he could, but he didn't see any hope for repairing the marriage. He just wanted to get an amicable divorce and get on with his life. Jim was clear that he was not leaving his children. In fact, he had been toying with the idea of going for sole custody because he felt his wife wasn't as stable a parent as he was. But he realized what this would do to her emotionally and he didn't really wish her harm.

He too was sad and confused, less angry than Janet but very guilty. He wished he knew how to salvage some semblance of a relationship with his wife and children. He worried the children would hate him and blame him for breaking up the family and that his wife might try to turn them against him. She had a friend who was really bitter about her own divorce and he believed this friend might influence Janet to be rigid and uncompromising.

The children came in the following week. Michael, age twelve, was just beginning to look like an adolescent. He had a certain bravado about him, a determination to appear cool and uncaring. He was angry at his father for hurting his mother. He wasn't sure what was going on but he knew they were in trouble.

Donna, ten, had freckles and a face that would someday be considered beautiful. She also had about her a sadness so powerful it could almost be touched. She was very scared of her parents' behavior. She knew they were talking about a divorce because she woke up one night and heard them arguing. She told me she was praying as hard as she could that they wouldn't do it and couldn't tell anyone her secret because that would make it feel too real. As long as they didn't tell her, she believed it might all go away. Then she'd feel safe again and finally able to sleep without bad dreams.

And there was Andy, a rambunctious, fidgety six-year-old with a nervous smile and bristly blond hair. He said he didn't really know why everyone was acting so weird lately. Nobody would talk about it but he knew stuff was going on. His dad acted angry all the time and was hardly ever home. His mom never smiled any more and was too tired to do anything with him. His brother and sister stayed in their rooms all the time and yelled at him if he came in to play. He sure wished someone would tell him what was going on so he wouldn't be so worried.

The first session with Jim and Janet together seemed to start with an optimistic feel. Both were calm and considerate, although cautious and clearly uncomfortable. We focused on what they wanted to do at this point. Was there a possible starting point for working on the marriage?

When Janet said that she still loved him and wanted to try to make things work, Jim's face froze. He looked away from her and said in a quiet monotone, "I'm in love with someone else and I want a divorce."

Janet looked like she had been slapped in the face. For several minutes she cried raggedly and no one spoke. Then, as her tears subsided, she began to scream at Jim about his lies, his unfaithfulness, and her own stupidity for loving him. Finally she got up, glared at him, and shouted, "I'm going to see that you never see the children. I'm going to bankrupt you if I can. You'll be sorry you ever met that bitch."

Then Jim jumped up too. "I was trying to make this easy on you but if you try to use the kids, I'm going to fight you for custody and with your history of depression, I think I'll win!"

Janet stormed out of the office. Jim turned to me. "I guess we won't be needing your services after all," he said. "You'll probably be hearing from my attorney. We're filing papers tomorrow."

Divorce never occurs in a vacuum, and it never occurs overnight. It doesn't happen just because one spouse becomes angry or fed up and decides to visit a lawyer's office.

Divorce is the end result of years of dissatisfaction, unhappiness, and conflict within a relationship. It may occur because the partners were not well suited for each other in the beginning, or because one outgrows the other emotionally. It may occur because the couple's relationship simply could not stay flexible enough to deal with the stresses of parenthood, jobs, or growing older.

Most people don't act impulsively when these feelings begin. Many put off the decision for years. Some try to get their spouses to join them in marital therapy. Others hold their pain secretly within, only to become more sullen or impatient as time goes on.

When couples divorce, attorneys see most of the anger and desire for revenge. As therapists, we usually see a mixture of the pain, sadness, and frustration that have accumulated over the years. What is it about the experience of loving that produces such pain and anger when it turns sour? How can people stay in a marriage for years to "protect" the children, then later try to turn the children against the other parent? To answer these questions you first need to understand certain basic principles.

# THE FOUR BASIC PRINCIPLES OF DIVORCE

To achieve a healthy divorce, it's important to review the past, reflect on the present, and consider the future. Look back over your relationship and understand the kinds of things that made you sad, discouraged, or angry. Then look at the present and try to recognize the effect that divorce will have on you, your children, and the rest of your family. In other words, before you take any action, step back and draw a picture in your mind, or write your reflections in a personal journal, of how you got to this place and where you need to go. As you attempt to understand divorce and its potential effects on your life, use the four basic principles to guide your reflections.

### Principles of the Divorce Experience

1. Divorce is the end result of years of unhappiness.

2. Spouses rarely decide to divorce at the same time. There is the one who leaves and the one who is left.

3. Staying together for the sake of the children does not work.

4. Divorce is like a death for parents and children.

## PRINCIPLE 1: DIVORCE IS THE END RESULT OF YEARS OF UNHAPPINESS.

If you are considering a divorce, ask yourself why you are planning it now and not several years ago. What has pushed you further away from the relationship? Think back over the years. Look at the Emotional Checklist and mark off anything that you've felt in your marriage over the past year. Add others if necessary. (If you are doing this with your spouse, one of you can put checks in the left margin and the other in the right.) Remind yourself what you and your spouse have done to try to relieve these feelings and improve the relationship.

Then fill in the proportion of the effort you believe each of you has put into improving the relationship over the past year. For example, if you are both working in marital therapy then the proportion would probably be fifty-fifty. If not, you may feel you've put in 80 percent of the effort while your spouse has contributed only 20 percent . There is no "right" answer; it's just a way of understanding what has been going on in your relationship.

## Appraising Your Marriage:
## An Emotional Checklist

Have you felt any of these emotions in your marriage in the past year?

- ☐ Confusion
- ☐ Disappointment
- ☐ Frustration
- ☐ Anger
- ☐ Rage
- ☐ Sadness
- ☐ Embarrassment
- ☐ Loneliness
- ☐ Hurt
- ☐ Regret
- ☐ Jealousy
- ☐ _____
- ☐ _____
- ☐ _____

Proportion of energy put into the relationship in past year:

Wife_____% Husband_____%

Many spouses will say something like this: "I gave up on this marriage eight years ago but I didn't know how to leave." If asked why not, they may give reasons such as:

"I didn't want to hurt the children."

"I grew up in a divorced family and I couldn't put the children through that."

"I couldn't deprive them of their father."

"I was afraid my mom and dad would not approve."

"I wasn't sure I could make it on my own."

"I didn't know if I would ever find anyone else."

"I always thought my unhappiness would go away."

Remember, divorces rarely occur suddenly or impulsively. They are the result of years of struggles that never seem to improve. The first step in understanding why you are considering a divorce is to look openly and honestly at your feelings and understand how they have brought you to this place. The next best step is to share these feelings with your spouse. If you don't think you can do that, then find an experienced family therapist who can create a safe and constructive experience for both of you to look at the relationship.

We always tell our clients who are considering divorce: "Whether you stay together or not, you need to understand why this relationship has failed so that you can either repair it or be sure not to carry the same issues into your next relationship."

## PRINCIPLE 2: SPOUSES RARELY DECIDE TO DIVORCE AT THE SAME TIME. THERE IS USUALLY THE ONE WHO LEAVES AND THE ONE WHO IS LEFT.

Divorce does not usually occur by consensus. One person usually begins to move away from the other. Even people who have been married only a few years and have no children rarely sit down and mutually agree to get a divorce.

There are many reasons for this. People in relationships that are not working well tend to be somewhat rigid in their roles and in their expectations for each other. When one spouse becomes uncomfortable or begins to outgrow that role, the change typically begins internally and may grow privately for some time. That person is often reluctant to openly express these early dissatisfactions and risk upsetting the partner and the balance in the relationship. Also, the communications in unsatisfactory relationships are usually poor. So even when one partner attempts to express concerns they may not be stated clearly or they may fall on deaf ears. The result is that one partner's dissatisfaction continues to grow while the other partner continues to be unaware.

Some couples get stuck in a vicious cycle in which their mixed feelings first push them toward divorce, then cause them to pull back. Spouses may even change roles in this cycle. First the wife moves closer to divorce and retreats, then months later the husband moves closer to divorce and pulls back. Many different issues may cause this fluctuation of feelings. A man may become very dependent on the marriage and the family for security and identity. Either person may have a genuine fear of what a single life, particularly as a parent, would really be like. And often, for women especially, there is the very real fear of financial disaster. Studies show that women have a far greater struggle to reestablish themselves financially after divorce than men.

In any case there are two distinct roles in most divorces: the one who is leaving and the one who is being left. Typically the one who is leaving carries a sense of guilt for "destroying" the family. That's often why this step is put off for years. The one who is being left carries a shattered sense of self-esteem and much of the anger and hurt. Studies show that the person who is left has more difficulty adjusting after the divorce than the one who is leaving, and is more susceptible to hanging on to the relationship and the anger.

This common pattern makes it difficult for couples to talk amicably about ending their relationship and to look together at the difficult decisions that need to be made about children, property, and finances. This emotional imbalance makes every divorcing couple susceptible to creating an adversarial process that requires the use of attorneys. Later we will discuss how this emotional dynamic sets the stage for unnecessary court battles, and how the legal and judicial systems fail to recognize the special needs of children and families by allowing these disputes to be escalated in our adversarial legal system.

If you are the one who is pursuing the divorce, you should not expect your partner to understand your reasons or accept your decision. You may have carried those feelings of dissatisfaction around for many years, mentioning them only occasionally. At the same time you may have withdrawn some of your attachment and loyalty to the marriage and given up your need to keep the family together. But even though there may have been great conflict in the marriage, your partner may still be as emotionally attached and loyal to you as you were to your partner before these feelings began.

To make this a healthier experience for you and your children, try to be patient with your spouse's anger and hurt. It may serve you well in the long run to slow down the process of the divorce and give your spouse time to catch up and accept the reality of your decision.

On the other hand, if you are the one who is being left, you're probably filled with many questions: Why? What happened? How could this happen? I thought everything seemed to be OK. You may ask what can be done to change your partner's mind, such as suggesting counseling. You may also have suspicions that your partner is involved with someone else, because "that's the only way you could decide to leave this suddenly."

Try to recognize that your partner has probably been much more unhappy than you realized for a number of years. Perhaps nothing much was really said to you, or maybe you rejected the signals because they were too scary. Perhaps you really knew but tried to ignore the obvious signs, hoping that the problem would go away if you didn't say anything. Or maybe you thought that if you just kept trying, eventually the problem would work itself out. You'll have to struggle through this process over the next few months or even years, knowing that your spouse has been struggling with it for a longer time and is much further down the road emotionally.

This will also make you angry. It may seem that your spouse doesn't care about you or the children because his pain, or hers, is less apparent. Try to understand that your partner's feelings have been underground and that your spouse has already done some of the work of detaching and healing. Your task is to understand your anger and resentment, accept the need to let go of the relationship, and begin to plan a future for yourself.

It takes both partners to make a marriage work. You can't do it all by yourself and hanging on will only increase the pain for everyone. Remember, there really is life after divorce, even though right now that may be hard to believe.

## PRINCIPLE 3: STAYING TOGETHER FOR THE SAKE OF THE CHILDREN DOES NOT WORK.

How often have you heard, "Don't divorce. Stay together for the sake of the children"? You'd probably be amazed to know how often we've heard children say, "I used to pray they'd get a divorce" or "I just wish they would get a divorce and stop fighting so much."

Of course, most children do not want their parents to divorce. But research strongly supports the conclusion that it is far more damaging for children to live in an unhappy home filled with tension, anger, manipulation, and a lack of affection than to go through the transitions of a divorce. It's likely, moreover, that after a period of adjustment, they will have healthier, happier, more competent, and stronger parents.

Yes, divorce is disruptive, painful, and confusing for all. But if the unhappiness in a marriage simply can't be improved and if the parents have tried for years to make it work without success, then divorce may be better for children than living in a home without love, without a model for a healthy, loving marriage, and without any end in sight to the bickering and the bitter cold of a marriage long dead.

We do not recommend divorce as an easy out for unhappiness. We believe that all avenues to remedy the rift should be explored, especially marital therapy. But if all has failed, you are not doing the children a favor by trapping them in a home without love.

## PRINCIPLE 4: DIVORCE IS LIKE A DEATH FOR PARENTS AND CHILDREN.

Many experts believe divorce is the second most traumatic life event that can occur, after the death of a child or parent. Divorce requires a person to grieve many losses, obvious and not so obvious. Your dreams for the future of your family must be laid to rest. Your hopes and expectations for the presence of your spouse in your continuing life must also be abandoned. When you divorce you must bury a relationship that once gave you love, security, stability, identity, dreams, and hope. Often, you leave behind a more comfortable lifestyle and must adjust to one filled with greater deprivation and financial struggles.

It's important to realize that getting over a divorce takes a great deal of time. It requires tremendous personal adjustments for both parents and children. It takes about two years, on average, to return to some semblance of predivorce emotional adjustment, but it can often take much longer. Allowing yourself to grieve is a very important part of that adjustment. Giving yourself permission to cry openly and frequently, even setting aside some time for wallowing in self-pity, will help you let go of the past and embrace the future when your grieving is complete.

Unfortunately, many people try their best to deny their grief and pretend they are just fine. Some jump immediately into a new relationship to protect themselves from feeling pain or loneliness. Others throw themselves into parenting, social activities, work, or alcohol or drugs to deny and push aside their pain. We believe that it's very important to feel and express your pain and be patient with yourself in the process. Using new loves or overinvolvement in activities to ward off the demons of your pain will come back to haunt you somewhere down the road. The divorce rate for second marriages is considerably higher than for first marriages, partly due to people's tendency to dive into new relationships long before they have sufficiently grieved their initial loss.

You must realize that, with a divorce, you are leaving behind the family structure that was and never can be again. New structures will take its place—often healthier, stronger, happier ones. But both parents and children must allow the old one to die before these newer ones can emerge. Learn to live alone and be alone, and get to a place where you like and enjoy this before you replace the silence with a new partner. Make friends with yourself and let this crisis strengthen and refine you before you reemerge into the world of new relationships. Many people have told us:

"This was the worst thing I've ever gone through but I'm so thankful for all the changes it forced on me."

"I didn't think I would ever be happy again but now it's as if life opened up for me and became fresh and new."

"I didn't think I would ever stop crying but when I finally did, I found the most wonderful person I've ever known."

## THREE TASKS TO ACCOMPLISH FOR A HEALTHY DIVORCE

When we talk to families about divorce, we try to define the experience as an ongoing process with certain predictable stages. Many people think of divorce only in terms of its most dramatic aspects, such as getting separated, talking to an attorney, or going to court. We would like you to step back and look at divorce as an emotional process that spans many years and may affect several generations of family members. The more all family members can understand, in their own terms, how they got to this place and where they are heading, the greater will be their potential for achieving a healthy divorce.

We explain to families that they must accomplish three main tasks: letting go, developing new social ties, and redefining parental roles.

### Three Tasks to Accomplish for a Healthy Divorce

1. Letting go

2. Developing new social ties

3. Redefining parental roles

### LETTING GO

This first stage is the *most critical* for a satisfactory and healthy resolution of the divorce experience. You must learn to let go of the attachment, caring, and loyalty to your former lover and partner.

For many people this process of disengagement or uncoupling can be very painful even though they may be feeling great frustration and anger. As therapists we have a word to describe this—*ambivalence*. It means simply that you experience both positive and negative feelings for the same individual. Sometimes the positive feelings will be stronger, other times the negative feelings will be stronger. Feeling ambivalent is a normal experience in letting go of a relationship, as we shall discuss in the next chapter.

Children also go through a type of disengaging process, though theirs is more difficult to define for themselves. Remember that children do not let go of their parents. But they must adjust to tremendous changes in the loss of their family structure.

Children must be helped to understand that the family system will undergo dramatic changes, that what they knew as their family, where both parents did things with them together, will no longer exist. They must be helped to see that they are now part of two new family systems, each headed by one parent only, and that these systems function independently of the other. They must let go of the belief that the former family structure will continue after separation and divorce. They must let go of trying to get the parents to reunite and accept the finality of the parents' decision to divorce.

The children's experience of letting go of the family is perhaps more difficult than the parents' process. It is often complicated because a parent who is struggling with letting go may be fueling the children's feelings of not letting go.

We often see people who are still hanging on emotionally to their former partner five and even ten years after a divorce. Even if they've remarried during that period, their continuing emotional attachment to the former spouse hinders their relationship with their new spouse. Remember, anger and resentment indicate as much of an emotional attachment as caring and loving.

Some men are especially susceptible to hanging on, particularly those who felt both dependent on their partner and also jealously possessive. One man was referred to Craig for therapy by his physician, who had watched him become more and more depressed and lose considerable weight over the year since his divorce had been finalized.

John was a short, slender fellow with sunken eyes and a dejected demeanor. The folds of skin around his chin and neck were indicators of the more than fifty pounds he had lost. He was still functioning adequately at his business because he was able to throw himself into his work. In fact he had done this throughout his former marriage; his wife had accused him of being a workaholic. The marriage had been childless, and since the divorce his personal life was nonexistent. He simply vegetated in his townhouse without friends or social life.

His wife had left him and gone to live with his friend and former business partner. He had depended on her to make his life comfortable and happy, to supply the social contacts he never pursued on his own, and to be an exclusive sexual partner. The sense of loss and rage he carried inside had immobilized him.

When John first came in it was fourteen months after the divorce. He had talked to his former wife about once a month during that period. These conversations began with anger and threats, then changed to crying and pleas for her return.

John had created an elaborate fantasy that it was just a matter of time before she would recognize the error of leaving him, realize that the guy she was living with was a jerk and come back home. He imagined that she would knock at his door late one night asking him to take her back. The fantasy became so powerful that for the past four months John had come home from work early each day and never went out on weekends because he did not want to risk being away from home when she returned.

It took John several months to work through the anger and loss and gradually begin to let go. Eventually therapy helped him to learn some things about his dependent and workaholic lifestyle and to believe he could look for more balanced companionship in his next relationship.

While this may seem a fairly dramatic example, it's really not uncommon. Achieving a successful divorce involves recognizing that the former marital bonds, commitments, and responsibilities are over. Loyalties to the relationship must be withdrawn and you must learn how to walk away.

## DEVELOPING NEW SOCIAL TIES

The second task is an ongoing process: reestablishing supportive relationships with your family of origin and building a social network to help with your adjustment as a single adult. When you begin to let go of your marital partner, this natural process of developing new social and emotional networks begins.

As you leave your marriage, a vacuum is often created. Your family is gone, and now friends seem to disappear too. Often some of the friends you had as a couple don't know how to continue with you as a single friend (see Chapter Seven). Others may have taken sides. Or you may have focused many years of energy on your immediate family and children, not needing to keep up with old friends or even parents and siblings. Whatever the reason, suddenly you are faced with one of your worst fears—being alone.

As you saw in John's case, it's dangerous and debilitating to become socially isolated. You must also be careful not to rely on your children, no matter what their ages, to satisfy your need for social contact and companionship.

You must also avoid throwing yourself into a new romantic relationship before you've gained some distance and healing from the divorce. Most new relationships that occur during or right after a divorce are called transitional relationships. This means that they are like a bridge, helping you get from one place to another. They are not necessarily bad; in fact they can be useful in helping to see yourself as a single person again, renewing your self-esteem and self-confidence. The error many people make is assuming that they're ready to turn these transitional relationships into permanent relationships. This happens because they are not used to being alone. The need to fill in the emotional vacuum with new companionship and affection is great. Unfortunately for many, these relationships are based more on a fear of being alone than on a solid basis for a new partnership.

Take your time! We see as clients too many people who remarried within six months after a divorce without looking carefully at the person they selected to marry or at their own needs. A hasty marriage can become a painful disaster for you and your children. If you are tempted to do this, at least see a marital therapist who can help you understand why your prior marriage failed and what elements of that experience you may be carrying into a new relationship.

Take your time! Give yourself a year or more to build a new social network—to see who you are now, how you relate, what dating is like, what you really want for your new life, and what you need from a new partner for yourself and your children. Look up old high school friends or people you used to work with. Reestablish ties and activities with your brothers and sisters. Don't be afraid to seek support from your parents, but keep some adult boundaries: if you go home again, you don't want to return as a child.

## REDEFINING PARENTAL ROLES

One of children's greatest fears is that they'll lose one or both of their parents. This is often reinforced after a divorce because both parents are typically angry at each other and their interactions are characterized by avoidance or conflict. Redefining parental roles with your former spouse is the third necessary step in the divorce process.

We tell our clients that one of the most difficult tasks facing them will be to learn to be parents when you are no longer lovers and partners. Some people do everything they can, with the help of their attorney, to push the other parent away or prevent a continuing role with the children. Studies show that the single most important factor influencing children's adjustment following divorce is their frequent and continuing interaction with both parents. And the second most important factor is the parents' ability to give up their animosity and instead begin to co-parent effectively.

To achieve a healthy divorce, you and your former spouse must reconnect and redefine your relationship as co-parents, no matter what form of custody you may have. This means learning to share time and responsibilities for the children and respecting the children's right and need to be with the other parent.

It means figuring out with each other—*not with the children as go-betweens*—how both of you can be present at your child's school play or soccer game, or how to coordinate teachers' meetings, birthdays, and holidays. It also means protecting your children's ongoing relationships with all their grandparents, aunts, uncles, and cousins. This may also involve reminding your own relatives that your children need their neutral support, not the rehashing of why Mom and Dad got divorced.

The goal here is to create a new family system for yourself and the children. At first it will be like two split families, each headed by a single parent. The children will have to learn how to move successfully between these two new systems. Later, spouses will probably remarry and create new family systems called blended families or stepfamilies. These will recreate the former family structure but with a different set of parents in charge and a new set of rules, expectations, and histories for the children to adjust to. These new adjustments will mark the final stages in the continuum of the divorce process. The more effectively you and your new co-parent can make this recoupling a consistent and supportive process, the more confident you can be that the children will make a long-term healthy adjustment.

We have given you a lot of information in this chapter to think about. We hope it will provide you with a foundation for understanding the kinds of emotional issues that occur in a divorce.

The four principles are practical information that we share with all of our clients who are considering divorce. They are intended to help you face the major issues that all divorcing spouses must struggle with.

The three tasks of a healthy divorce represent the most crucial elements in working through the ending of a relationship, gaining a sense of closure, and going on with your life as an individual and a parent. The themes from these three stages will appear throughout the rest of the book.

In the chapters ahead we consider the fourteen stages in the divorce process. These chapters will take you step by step through the continuum of a divorce and give you guidelines on what to expect and steps you can take to help everyone—parents and children—achieve a healthy divorce.

# 2

# Early Warning Signs

**B**EFORE PEOPLE EVEN BEGIN to think about a divorce there are usually early warning signs that indicate their growing dissatisfaction and unhappiness with the relationship.

The most common factor that pushes a person closer to divorce is a sense that things will not change for the better. Most people can live with a normal range of ups and downs over the course of their marriage. And most people have an inherent optimism, at least early in a relationship. They want to believe that things can get better. It's only after many attempts to improve the situation have been made, often including marital therapy, that a lingering sense of hopelessness sets in and people begin to see and expect the worst in their partner.

Let's take a look at the early warning signs. This chapter is about the first two stages. It will help you understand how the process toward divorce can begin and also evaluate whether there are windows of opportunity to alter that course.

## STAGE 1
## CLOUDS OF DOUBT

In the last chapter we saw how ambivalence can cause a confusing mixture of positive and negative feelings toward your partner. This is the earliest indication of a gradual erosion in a relationship. You begin to experience more and more doubts about who your partner really is, what originally attracted you, and whether you really want to stay with that person forever.

You may express more anger toward your partner about things that were previously left unsaid. You may begin to test the limits, as a child would, seeing how far you can push your spouse in the hope that something might change or at least that your unhappiness will be noticed. You may do things that you've never done before, like spending more money on yourself or going out evenings with friends without your spouse. You may begin to have fantasies such as:

Getting on a plane and just leaving

Pursuing an old high school sweetheart you've often fantasized about

Being swept off your feet and carried away by the perfect lover

Imagining your spouse being killed suddenly in an automobile accident

You may not be comfortable with these feelings, behaviors, or fantasies, but they are clear indicators that your hopes of having a better marriage are disappearing. The confusing part about this stage of heightened ambivalence is that you may experience many of these feelings strongly for a few days, then all of a sudden wake up with a renewed determination to make the marriage work and to see the better side of your partner. That's the way it was with Laurie and Tom.

Laurie, a woman in her mid thirties with a pale face and haggard appearance, told Sandy she didn't know why but she felt unhappy all the time, especially when she was at home. She described her marriage of fifteen years as having its ups and downs but said it had seemed empty for several years. She had tried everything she could think of to revive her feelings for her husband, Tom, but everything she tried seemed to work for only a few days, then the usual pattern of being angry with him for minor things and feeling bored with their life together would return. She felt as if life was passing her by and she was getting old before her time.

Laurie thought Tom seemed confused and unsympathetic to her complaints. He told her he thought their life together was fine, and he couldn't understand why she was always complaining and unhappy. She said she needed more from him—more time, more romance, more communication. She confided that she often thought of just leaving one day, packing her boys into the car and escaping to another city where no one would know her. The only times she enjoyed were when she was at work or out with her two girlfriends, something she was beginning to do more often. She was also beginning to notice apartment ads in the paper and think about how to divide their furniture.

Laurie and Tom were at a very precarious place in their relationship. She needed to convince Tom to come in and talk about her unhappiness before she took the next step of convincing herself that the only answer was to separate or divorce.

Tom did agree to come in. Although it was difficult for him at first, he finally began to understand that their marriage was in trouble and that they both would have to make some significant changes to get it back on track. He began to take Laurie out more and to be more attentive and romantic. He learned to communicate with her about her unhappiness without feeling threatened or defensive. And he learned to take the cues of her ambivalence as a serious sign that changes needed to be accomplished. Laurie and Tom responded to these early warning signs and were able to repair their marriage without moving closer to divorce.

## THE CHILDREN'S EXPERIENCE

This first stage of beginning doubt is also when the children become aware that problems between their parents may be more serious than just normal arguments. The children may feel increased tension and instability and become more cautious when new and unpredictable behaviors occur. Some children may pull away from the parents as a way of managing their new anxiety. Others may become more clinging and dependent in an effort to reassure themselves that everything is still normal.

At this early stage, children can become acutely and intuitively aware that something is different about the way their parents are behaving toward each other. Some children see their parents' unhappiness as a sign that the parents don't love them as much. They may begin to act out their fear, which often leads to intensified arguments between the parents about managing the children's behavior. These arguments often form the basis for the later guilt children can feel when the parents announce they are separating or divorcing. The children feel responsible, since it appeared that their being in trouble was what the parents were always fighting about.

Timmy was seven when he was referred to us by his teacher. He had suddenly become aggressive with his peers, had stopped doing his schoolwork, and had an "attitude" in the classroom. At home, the parents noticed that he seemed quieter and more withdrawn, that he cried easily and for little reason. The parents frequently argued over how to discipline him for his acting out in school.

When we first met, Timmy was subdued; he seemed to be waiting to be punished. He was confused about why the teacher was always mad at him. He couldn't say why he was so sad although he was aware that he didn't feel happy very often. When asked about how things were in the family, he tried to avoid talking and began to play with toys in the office in an increasingly destructive way. In his play, however, he recreated his family with small dollhouse figures. Here the parents were arguing a lot and the dad was always going out, which made the mom yell even more.

Timmy thought his parents' lack of emotional warmth meant they didn't love him as much as before. He believed his father was staying away from home more because he was so bad. He finally whispered a "secret" that he made us promise not to tell his parents: "I'm afraid my parents are going to get a divorce."

His secret fear and anxiety were leading to Timmy's difficulties at home and at school. The parents were amazed that Timmy was thinking of this since they had never spoken of their difficulties around him. Eventually, this concern for their child led them to engage in marital therapy.

If you or your spouse are struggling with this ambivalent stage, your thoughts are going to be filled with your own unhappiness. But you must save some energy to help your children. Never underestimate your children's awareness of your tension and their fear of your getting divorced. With the prevalence of divorce today, it's highly likely that your child has many friends whose parents were divorced. They've probably heard stories of their friends visiting both of their parents' homes or about one parent getting married again. Children often don't share this knowledge or anxiety with their parents, partly because they're afraid their fears will be confirmed.

If your child does share this fear with you, be careful how you respond. Parents are often surprised when a child asks if they are getting a divorce and may reply with an emphatic *no*. Don't pretend things are fine when they are not, and don't increase their fear with an overly vague answer. Instead, try something like this: "Daddy (or Mommy) and I have been having some problems lately that we're trying hard to work out and I'm sorry that's worrying you so much. But we have not talked about a divorce and I really hope that things will be better soon."

Jennifer, age eight, knew something was very wrong with her parents. She was an unusually verbal child with shiny black hair and a solemn face.

> It seems like they fight about the stupidest things. Even when they're not fighting, they hardly ever talk nicely to each other any more. Sometimes I see my mom crying but she won't tell me why. I get really scared that my dad might not come home some night. I try to be extra good but no one seems to care if I'm good or not any more. I can't even ask them what's wrong because they give each other these mean looks and say nothing. But I know they're lying.

Jennifer's fears and fantasies are typical of most children whose parents are moving toward divorce. Some children express these fears as anger and they begin to withdraw from the painful family experience. Billy, age ten, told me:

> I don't know what their problem is but I'm sick of it. We never do stuff together any more. And hardly anyone talks to anyone any more. I try to stay over at my friend's house any time I can. At least his parents aren't always fighting and mean to each other.

Other children, such as five-year-old Cynthia, express their fears through tears and sadness:

> Sometimes I cry at night after they tuck me in. I'm really scared but I don't know what about. Mommy and Daddy are acting really weird and nobody tells me anything. They think I'm too little. I'm not little any more and I wish somebody would tell me what's going on.

Above all, encourage your children to talk about what they're feeling. If they have difficulty sharing these feelings with you, find them an experienced child and family therapist. Often the loyalties that most children feel toward each parent prevent them from sharing their fears with you. However, when these fears are kept inside they can lead to problems at school, at home, and with peers.

## DEALING WITH EARLY DOUBTS

The main task for couples at this early stage is to focus on what the relationship was like before children and life stresses began to intrude into the romance. Sometimes you need to go back to courtship days and remember the early excitement and romance.

Couples often forget what they liked about each other in the beginning of their relationship, what glue began to bind them together. When spouses become ambivalent, it is an early warning sign that they are less close, less committed, and less happy. They need to confront the issues that have created these changes. Spouses can benefit from more private time away from their children and family, renewing their feelings of being lovers and friends. If caught early, this stage can startle the couple into working on their relationship with renewed energy and commitment. It requires more investment of time, patience, communication, and caring on both sides.

Children often are aware of this early stage at more of an intuitive than a cognitive level. Their main task is to try to talk about their feelings of worry or insecurity and to verbalize what their "guts" are telling them. It's important that they try to give their parents their privacy, to encourage their parents to go out without them so they can get closer and work out their differences with each other. Of course, this is easier for older children to accomplish than younger, more dependent ones.

---

# STAGE 2
# THE COLD SHOULDER

The doubt and ambivalence we have just described often begin to be more obvious in a variety of distancing behaviors. The spouse who is more dissatisfied begins to pull away from the marriage and do more separate and independent activities.

If this spouse (let's say it's the wife) suspects that the children and other family members will disapprove of her unhappiness with the marriage and of the possibility of a divorce, then she may begin to move away from these family ties too. She may make friends with people who are recently divorced, believing that they are the only ones she can safely share her doubts and unhappiness with. Gradually she withdraws positive feelings, attachments, and loyalties from her partner.

Usually this distancing occurs over a period of at least a year but may extend over many years. As positive regard is withdrawn from a relationship, the next step is that people become emotionally and physically unavailable to their partner. This means that the unhappy spouse does not respond to a hug or a kiss, and becomes uninterested and unresponsive sexually. This evokes angry interactions as hurt feelings begin to accumulate, creating even more intense arguments.

Remember that family systems typically survive by maintaining a sense of balance. As one spouse's doubts and distancing increase in a relationship, the imbalance begins to affect the entire system. Imagine yourself as a child playing with a friend on a seesaw. If you both maintain the balance you can easily move up and down. But if suddenly your friend jumps off, you'll crash to the ground. And you'll usually be very angry that you have!

This is what happens when one partner distances from the relationship. Even if this process is never discussed, your partner will sense—at first emotionally, later cognitively—that you are less available and less responsive. Something will begin to feel out of balance and your partner will try to restore the balance by reaching out to you more, perhaps becoming more playful, more attentive, more generous, more romantic. You may respond to this at first because it renews your sense of hope. But if you don't respond to your partner's efforts to rebalance the relationship, the gestures may become more demanding, angry and then threatening. As you move further toward the next stage of separation, these responses may turn to tearful pleas, offers to go to counseling with you, and guilt-producing manipulations. This may even involve efforts to recruit the children to pull you back into the relationship.

Linda and Howard were experiencing the back-and-forth shifts. Linda was a petite, energetic woman who was very devoted to her family. Howard was a quiet country boy from Louisiana who was shy and awkward with strangers. They had been married ten years and had two children. Most of their relationship had been fairly stable, though Linda acknowledged later that she had been unhappy in the relationship for the last five years and on a few occasions had thought about separating. Howard had refused to go to marriage enrichment classes or pursue marital therapy, saying, "That's stupid; we don't need anybody helping us."

Six months before they were referred to us for therapy, Linda had begun to push on the normal limits of her role in the relationship. She told Howard that she had joined a karate class to exercise and learn self-discipline. A few weeks later she announced that on Friday nights she would be going out for a few hours after work with girlfriends and he would be responsible for the kids. She planned a trip alone, without Howard or the kids, to Ohio to visit her sister—the first time she had ever traveled by herself.

All these changes were disturbing to Howard. They upset the normal balance of roles they had established over the past ten years. He still didn't believe that anything was wrong with the relationship. But he began to believe that Linda could benefit from therapy because she was certainly "acting weird."

The most dramatic change occurred when Linda became more sexually aggressive with Howard. Over the years he had been the one to initiate sex most of the time. Now, not only was she initiating more sex but she was wanting to try new positions and even asked him to make love one night on their front porch after the children were in bed. He agreed to come in for marital therapy the next week.

## EXTRAMARITAL RELATIONSHIPS

As the distancing increases, the potential for extramarital affairs also increases. Until this point, the unhappy spouses probably never even imagined having an affair. However, once the distancing stage is reached, they may pursue other relationships, for a variety of reasons:

1. To prove to themselves they are still likable and attractive

2. To prove they are still sexually desirable

3. To create a sense of excitement and adventure

4. To test their own personal boundaries by engaging in a "dangerous" liaison

5. To push on the limits of the marriage in an attempt to get their spouse's attention

There are some differences in how men and women respond to other relationships during this distancing stage. Women seem to be much more capable of pursuing a platonic, nonsexual friendship with a man—at least at first. Usually this is with someone at work or even a friend of her husband's. Such a relationship allows the wife to renew her sense of personal worth and gives her an opportunity to interact more openly with another adult in what may seem to be a safe friendship. It is of course sometimes true that these early friendships can turn into sexual relationships as her unhappiness increases.

Unfortunately, men have more difficulty seeking out or experiencing platonic friendships with women. It is perhaps a matter of both socialization and biology that men tend to view women, even through supportive friendships, as potential sexual companions. Therefore many men tend to seek primarily sexual liaisons at this distancing stage.

For both husbands and wives, the affairs that may occur at this stage are usually experimental and will not necessarily turn into committed relationships. They are symptoms of a deteriorating marriage but do not have to end the marriage if the partners can mend the growing rift.

*A word of caution:* If you are feeling very needy for companionship as you distance from your marriage, be careful not to imagine that the person you are attracted to is someone with magical powers who can rescue you from your unhappy state or take away all your sad and angry feelings. Take your time!

For example, consider Sarah and Bob. They had been married eight years. Bob was a serious fellow, often preoccupied, who worked hard for the phone company. Sarah was engaging and outgoing and worked in a manufacturing plant. Sarah had developed a friendship over the past two years with Mel, a co-worker, who was also married. Bob learned through friends that Sarah and Mel went to lunch together occasionally or out for drinks with other co-workers after work. Bob exploded, accusing Sarah of having an affair. Sarah tried unsuccessfully to assure Bob that this was a nonsexual friendship.

In therapy, Sarah reported that she had become increasingly unhappy with her marriage over the past five years. She felt Bob was less interested in doing things with her and that he had become less affectionate,

except sexually. She had even suggested that they go to a marital therapist two years earlier but he had refused. She also felt she enjoyed and
benefitted from the communication and interaction with Mel. She did,
however, acknowledge that she was beginning to have sexual fantasies
about the relationship but never considered acting on them.

Bob had great difficulty accepting Sarah's statement that this was
not a romantic or a sexual liaison. At first he became threatening and
potentially violent toward Mel and later threatened to have an affair
himself. But he did agree to join Sarah in marital therapy. He eventually recognized that she needed more personal attention and communication from him, and that this friendship with Mel was an early
warning sign.

## THE CHILDREN'S EXPERIENCE

Children become intuitively aware of distancing behaviors, but, they
will not usually talk about it. They may become confused by their parents' behaviors or messages but may be afraid to ask about what's
going on.

Children often begin to move away emotionally from the distancing
parent, aligning themselves with the other parent, who is more obviously distressed and hurt by the widening rift in the relationship. Frequently this alignment is fostered and reinforced by this parent, perhaps to compensate for a dependency not being met in the relationship with the distancing spouse. Sometimes it is reinforced as a
weapon to reduce the closeness between the child and the distancing
parent and to force more commitment and involvement from that parent. Often it may be fostered simply because the anxious and dis-
traught parent clings to the children as a way to escape fear of the
unknown, to feel more loved and needed.

Whatever the underlying reason, it's important that parents resist
the temptation to create these conflicts of loyalty or to force some sort
of alignment from their children. Otherwise this can result in serious
emotional damage for the children.

This was evident with Amy, a solemn seven-year-old who was trying to act much older, who sat in Sandy's office and declared: "I hate
my mother." When I asked about this, she said, "All my mother cares
about is going out and seeing her friend from work. She doesn't care

about us any more." When I asked what "us" she meant, she said "me and my dad. He told me he tries to get her to stay home but she does-n't care about us any more and all she wants to do is have a good time. He says we'll have to take care of ourselves and that he'll never leave me, like she is."

This child had been given her father's pain, hurt, and anger to carry as her own. He had fostered an alliance with her against the mother to get even with his wife for unbalancing the relationship and to validate his own unhappy perception of her behavior. The marriage might or might not endure, but the relationship between Amy and her mother was already severely damaged, which likely will create significant difficulties for this child for years to come.

To make the divorce experience as healthy as possible for your chil-dren, remember that even subtle changes in your behavior can disrupt their security and attachment. Be sensitive to their needs for stability and safety, and encourage them to express their concerns or fears to you or to a therapist.

## DEALING WITH DISTANCING

If you are the one who is distancing, try to help your spouse see the seriousness of your feelings. Don't be ambiguous. Don't try to take care of your partner's feelings or to avoid a confrontation. Your spouse has a right and a need to know what is really happening; it is the unknown that is so frightening and can cause the greatest damage in the long run. Be honest, be clear. Consider meeting with someone else—clergy, therapist, or friend. Try to *communicate* about what you need rather than *act out* what you need.

If you are the spouse who is becoming confused and frightened by the distancing of your partner, don't minimize what is happening or deny that it is real and potentially damaging. Listen to your spouse and take his or her issues seriously. Be willing to make changes even if they seem silly. Consider seeing a marital therapist together with your spouse to guide you in making the most beneficial changes.

And a word to both parents: Do not use your children either to soothe yourself or to hurt the other spouse. Your children are fragile. A great deal of damage can be done if you use them to play out your marital difficulties with each other. Do whatever you can to avoid establishing a climate where they feel pressured to take sides. Try to help them understand that there are always two sides to hurt feelings. It is much healthier for them not to take on your feelings as their own.

Recognize that the children are frightened. Encourage them to be with their friends a lot, stay active in lots of things, and talk to special friends about their feelings. Let them know this will help them feel less scared.

Also encourage them to talk to *you*, even though this means you will have to hear that what you are doing or saying is scaring your children. And let them know it's okay to see a counselor to help them with their feelings, that talking to someone outside the family can really help them feel better.

# 3

# The Process of Separating

A S THE DISTANCING SPOUSE moves further away from the relationship, the growing imbalance begins to produce more stress in the marital relationship and the parent-child relationships. This tension and agitation throughout the family provoke the gradual movement toward what we believe is the most dramatic and stunning aspect of the divorce process—the decision to physically separate. The next three stages reflect the experiences associated with this period of separation and transition.

## STAGE 3
## PRESEPARATION
## FANTASIES

As the marriage moves closer to physical separation, the distancing spouse, and to a lesser extent the spouse who is hanging onto the relationship, begin to experience what we call *preseparation fantasies and actions.* They begin to imagine what it would be like to live without each other, to escape from the family, or to get their emotional and physical needs met by other partners.

Some spouses imagine returning to the remembered safety of their hometowns and families of origin, even if these are thousands of miles away and they haven't lived there for many years. One of Sandy's clients, for example, daydreamed about a high school sweetheart that she had not seen since graduation. "We were at the twenty-fifth reunion and dancing to our favorite song. He invited me to go home with him that night."

Others imagine more adventurous escapes into fantasized sexual or romantic liaisons, often in glamorous places. One of Craig's clients imagined becoming an airline pilot. "I could travel to exotic places and make love to stewardesses on the beach every night." Still others consider more practical goals of returning to school or changing careers. Even parents who have no intention of giving up their children may fantasize about a new single lifestyle with a sense of relief and excitement.

These are not always limited to daydreams. The distancing spouse may actually act out these fantasies, either through extramarital relationships, as we discussed in the last chapter, or by going out of town more often—traveling more on the job or making more frequent excursions "back home." As these fantasies and actions begin to take a clearer form and more practical intent, they propel the spouse beyond the stage of ambivalence to a further withdrawal of loyalties from the partner and from the marriage bond.

This new experience of seeing yourself as separate and divorced carries with it a frightening reality: how to tell spouse, children, parents, extended family members, friends, and colleagues of the decision to leave the marriage.

## A QUESTION OF TIMING

Many spouses experience the potential reality of divorce as excruciating and therefore postpone the decision for years. They are worried that they may disappoint or alienate their parents and friends. Many struggle with fears of failure or loneliness, or the guilt of leaving their spouse and the obstacles involved in becoming a single parent. Carol's situation is typical.

Carol was a slightly overweight, tired-looking woman of forty. She told Craig she had made the decision to separate and divorce eight years ago, but she never announced her decision to anyone except one close female friend. "My children were only six and ten," she said, "and my parents are very religious. I knew they would say I had failed as a wife and mother."

When Carol was a teenager her parents had told her that she should be grateful they had stayed together for her sake and for her younger sister. Now she cried when she tried to imagine how she would tell her daughters, now eighteen and fourteen, of her decision.

During these eight years Carol had returned to school three times but quit, she said, because of no support from her husband and children. Despite her strong religious upbringing and the heavy sense of guilt in her family, she had also engaged in two brief sexual liaisons over the past two years. She had been in therapy for the past year and a half and had been treated with the antidepressant Prozac. As her depression lifted, she was finally ready to announce her intentions of leaving the marriage and wanted help in planning a healthy course of action.

Occasionally we see couples where both spouses have discussed or threatened separation over many years but have never taken any real actions toward doing so. While their relationships deteriorate further over these years, their choice to continue living together without getting any therapeutic help or taking any actions creates a clearly dysfunctional family environment for them and their children.

These couples become emotionally stuck, living in a sort of permanent standoff. In their mutual unhappiness, each is waiting for the other to take the first step. This can go on for years, with one threatening divorce and then backing away, then the other playing the same role. It becomes a circular dance, with both partners unhappy but too dependent and scared to walk away. The ones who eventually pursue help usually express a sense of relief that they can finally talk openly of their pain and the fears that have immobilized them over the years.

Sometimes we recommend that these "stuck" couples see a family-law attorney for an hour of education about the legal aspects of separation and divorce. This helps them think and plan more realistically about what is involved in this decision to be apart. After this some couples decide they are not ready to divorce and instead return to marital therapy with renewed commitment. Others decide that they are ready to go ahead and plan the separation and divorce.

If you and your partner decide to seek consultation with an attorney, be aware that many attorneys are not comfortable performing this educational role, especially with both spouses. Attorneys are trained in adversarial roles where their job is to fight for their client. So they of course cannot represent both of you.

You need to find an attorney who is willing to be a consultant only and not represent either of you if you ultimately pursue the divorce. Check with a local marital and family therapist or divorce mediator for such a referral. The attorney may ask you to sign a disclaimer indicating that she will not be representing you and is not giving you legal advice. This is an acceptable procedure; it protects her ethical obligations.

In contrast to the "stuck" spouse or couple, other people in this preseparation stage may be pulled too quickly toward the physical separation. The distancing spouse is often influenced toward separation by same-sex friends who have been through a divorce or by their parents or other family members. They often get messages like these:

"We told you it would never work."

"We never liked her from the beginning."

"I said he would never amount to anything."

"You'll be better off without her."

"We'll give you money for a good lawyer so he doesn't get the kids."

"You can come and live with us until this is over."

Here, as in the other stages, *take your time*. Make sure you are ready for the separation. Returning home to parents or moving in with friends is never a good option except in an emergency. The right timing and a careful process of transition are extremely important if you are to manage a healthy process toward divorce.

## CHILDREN AND PRESEPARATION FANTASIES

Children's fantasies at this stage are often consistent with those of the reluctant spouse. They fantasize peace and harmony returning, the magical ending of stress and anger, and the parents suddenly loving again. If they think about the possibility of separation and divorce (and most do), it is with fear and dread and frightful images of loss.

The fantasies of the family being fine again and the magical wish for stress to go away protects them to some degree from the pain of accepting the reality of what is actually happening. It helps them deny that anything too terrible is wrong and soothes them into overlooking some of the obvious cues of drastic changes. Although some level of soothing fantasies is comforting for children, too much denial and refusal to accept reality is not advisable. Giving the children accurate representations of what is happening in the family is important to their eventual adjustment. Don't reinforce their fantasies or try to create an unreal world where everything is OK and there's nothing for them to worry about. Their reaction to an eventual announcement that the parents plan to separate or divorce will be much more severe if they have been encouraged to create an unreal fantasy of a magical return to the former family functioning.

## STAGE 4
## THE SHOWDOWN: PHYSICAL SEPARATION

Of all the stages in the divorce process, the physical separation is the most dramatic and has the most far-reaching consequences for spouses, children, and the extended family. It takes the spouses and the children beyond the former ambivalence, worries, anticipation, dread, and fantasies to the actual physical breakup of the family. When one of the spouses moves out, there is no more pretending that life can go on as usual, no more denying the reality of the feelings of all involved.

Therefore it is *critical* that spouses take their time to plan carefully for the actual separation. The only exception to this is when violence or abuse is present. In most other cases, one of the worst things that you can do is separate too quickly or impulsively.

Many couples, even those in therapy, make the precipitous decision to separate after a major argument. When couples separate too quickly, they fail to consider the emotional and financial repercussions. They also fail to recognize the potential long-lasting effects on their children. To jump into an unplanned separation can overwhelm the already overburdened relationship and further aggravate anger and resentment. It will strain already difficult communications. We suspect that many divorces may have occurred simply because the separation was not planned carefully and the failure of the separation experience pushed the couple into the next step of actual divorce.

## TWO TYPES OF SEPARATION

We tell our clients that there are basically two types of separations:

1. An experimental separation to diffuse conflict, allow distance, and test the future of the relationship

2. A separation that represents a gradual transition into the divorce

The experimental separation buys the couple some time to step back and look more objectively at each other. It allows them, particularly the distancing spouse, to experiment with some limited independence and autonomy. It's particularly useful where there have been high levels of stress and conflict because it allows the intensity of emotions to ease and calmer feelings to emerge.

For couples who are not sure about pursuing a divorce but who cannot continue to live together, the experimental separation allows them some relief and the necessary space to gain some objectivity. They can start or continue in marital therapy. They can try to gain a new perspective on their relationship while understanding some of their own behaviors that have contributed to the deterioration of their relationship.

Couples considering this type of separation often ask us what the odds are they'll get back together. The best we can say is that the odds are fifty-fifty. The final outcome of such a separation depends on many variables, such as:

- The degree of ambivalence and distancing in the relationship
- The preparedness of the distancing spouse to be apart
- The levels of conflict and distrust that are present
- Each spouse's personal resources for communication and interaction

- Whether the couple is in therapy together during this time

We recommend that couples be in therapy jointly during an experimental separation. Often when a separation occurs, spouses will feel a need to seek individual therapy. It *is* important to attend to these individual concerns, but it's equally important for the couple to process and discuss the separation experience together with a therapist present. Often an experienced marital therapist can continue to see the spouses jointly as well as individually, so that a variety of needs can be met. Sometimes the therapist will refer each spouse to colleagues for individual sessions and will coordinate the types of sessions needed.

The second type of separation—a transition toward divorce—provides the couple who have made the decision to seek a divorce the necessary time and space to prepare themselves and their children for the divorce. It begins the specific decoupling and disengaging process that we discussed earlier.

All family members need time to process and accept the reality of the divorce. There is little to be gained and often a great deal to be lost by rushing into a divorce, especially if there are children involved.

## DISCUSSING LIVING ARRANGEMENTS

It's our experience that once a couple or spouse makes the decision to divorce, it is not realistic to continue living together in the same house. We have worked with many couples who have tried it, because of either emotional or financial reasons. It does not work! It will only bring more harm to your relationship and unnecessary stress for your children.

The underlying anger and fear in the divorce experience simply make it too hard for spouses to continue cordial or even civil interactions while living together after deciding to divorce. Inevitably the leftover marital conflict continues to be played out with more intensity and destructiveness. Even with one spouse sleeping in another bedroom, anger and hurt spread throughout the household. One parent often tries to develop alliances with the children against the other parent. Even everyday behaviors and routines become problematic and unsettling.

If you cannot realistically afford to be separated, then put off the divorce until you can. If you are not emotionally ready for the physical separation, then postpone it until you are. Timing is critical to making the best and healthiest choices for yourselves and your children.

Craig saw one couple who had made the decision to divorce about six months earlier but had stayed together to save money for lawyers' fees. The husband had been the distancer and had initiated the divorce after the couple had been in marital therapy for about a year. The wife had reluctantly accepted the decision to divorce, even though she carried a great deal of unspoken anger and hurt.

This couple was referred to us by one of their attorneys, who said that she would not work with them because they were so angry. She felt they could work out a more realistic divorce settlement if they could settle down emotionally. Both attorneys agreed that the children were being harmed by their current living arrangement.

Both the husband and wife told Craig they wanted to be seen individually because they couldn't be in the same room together. Since there was the likelihood that they would try to get him to take their respective sides, he insisted that both come in together.

When they arrived for the first session they were seething with anger and sat as far away from each other as possible. They did agree that continuing to live together had turned destructive and potentially violent. Each had attempted to turn the three children against the other. The resultant standoff had one son aligned with the father and the younger son and daughter aligned with the mother. The two sons had been in several physical fights in the prior two weeks. Routine communication between the spouses had turned to threats and manipulations in front of the children. About a month earlier the husband had broken into the wife's bedroom and tried to have sex with her forcibly.

Craig controlled this first session carefully so that the anger could be managed. He shifted their focus away from themselves and to the children. This diffused some of their anger and allowed them to be more objective about the choices and decisions they had to make. Ultimately they agreed to plan a constructive separation as a transition toward divorce, then to work on letting go of their anger and animosity. Meanwhile, Sandy saw the three children together to help them sort out their feelings and repair their relationships with one another. She began the process of helping them deal with their parents' decision to divorce and saw them intermittently over the next several months.

All spouses planning a separation also need to be aware of some legal issues. In states where divorce is characterized as "no fault"—meaning that the court and attorneys cannot define settlements on the basis of blame or fault—the act of separating cannot normally be used for or against either spouse. In other words, if you are the one who moves out of the house, that does not mean that you necessarily have to give up your right to the custody of the children or to your property.

If, however, there is so much animosity between you and your spouse that your partner may withhold or divert financial resources from the family or run up large debts in anger, then you may want to consult an attorney about a temporary assignment of custody and child support that would be in effect during the separation. This is referred to as *pendente lite* orders. Or you may want to consider a legal separation.

In some states the choice and pattern of a separation could potentially jeopardize your rights in the divorce or could be used against you. If you are uncertain about this, you should consult an attorney or mediator prior to a separation to protect your rights.

## A GUIDE TO PLANNING A HEALTHY PHYSICAL SEPARATION

Separation is a difficult and dramatic step for your family. We have seen many couples struggle with separations that actually became worse than their unhappy married life together. But we have also seen couples who have made separations work smoothly and constructively. Here are some suggestions to help you plan your separation.

### 1. Decide on the Goals of the Separation.

Is this a trial separation or a transition to divorce? You may not be ready to make a clear choice between the two types of separations that we have outlined. If you cannot define one of those directions, then proceed with the separation but agree that within a specified period of time a clearer goal will be defined.

## How to Plan a Healthy Separation

1. Decide on the goals of the separation.

2. Decide on a reasonable time limit for the separation.

3. Decide which spouse is going to move out.

4. Negotiate financial responsibilities during the separation.

5. Decide on a residential access plan for the children.

6. Decide how much time you want to spend with each other.

7. After everything is planned, tell the children.

### 2. Decide on a Reasonable Time Limit for the Separation.

Separations should be defined for a specific time period, generally between one month and one year. Separations are not effective if they are open ended, meaning that they go on and on until one person gets tired of it. And they're not helpful if they only last a few days or weeks. We usually recommend to our clients that they plan their separation in six- to eight-week segments. How you may feel one or two weeks into a separation is not a reliable way to make a lasting decision. Separation evokes many new feelings and perceptions, and people need time to experience them.

If we're seeing a separating couple, we review what the separation experience has been like for each of them at the end of eight weeks. We then suggest one of three options:

1. Continue the separation as is or with some modifications for another six to eight weeks.

2. Decide to discontinue the separation and make plans to reconcile with the eventual goal of moving back together again.

3. Redefine the separation with the intent of pursuing a divorce.

### 3. Decide Which Spouse Is Going to Move Out.

Be realistic. Consider the needs and stability of the children. It does not make much sense for a father who travels extensively in his work and is not available during daytime hours to insist on staying in the house. Nor is it appropriate for a mother who works only ten hours a week to move into a small apartment with three children. We have known some couples who have worked out an innovative plan where the children stay in the house and the parents alternate, one living in the house with the children for two weeks or a month at a time while the other lives in a nearby apartment, then the parents switch residences. This plan seems to work only with people who are able to get along well and are fairly flexible.

Be careful when considering the size and location of the second residence. If the separation is likely to be a long one, more than two or three months, it's important that the second residence not feel like a motel or a cramped closet. The children will resist visiting this type of place and the parent who moved there is likely to feel a great deal of resentment. Of course it may be financially unrealistic to duplicate the home situation, but it's important to provide a comfortable feeling and sufficient room to accommodate everyone for an extended period of time.

### 4. Negotiate Financial Responsibilities During the Separation.

Make a detailed budget. Don't kid yourself: it is more costly operating two households, even if one is a small apartment.

Define who is going to pay which bills, and how.

Define who will pay the children's needs such as clothes and school activities during the separation period.

### 5. Decide on a Residential Access Plan for the Children.

Where will the children reside during the school week and on weekends? *Be specific.*

Define specific days and times that they will live with the parent who is outside the household. How will transportation be shared?

Decide how to spend holidays, vacations, and birthdays that occur during the separation.

Ensure that the children will have access to all their grandparents and other extended family members whenever possible.

### 6. Decide How Much Time You Want to Spend with Each Other.

Schedule a time to have lunch or dinner together at least once each week. It is easier at first to spend time together out in public than in private.

Continue your marital therapy sessions.

Establish boundaries so you can truly experience being separate. Don't go to the other spouse's residence unannounced, and never go in when the other person is not there, unless you have advance permission.

If necessary, limit telephone calls to each other.

Don't spend nights together at the house. This will confuse the children.

Decide in advance whether you are going to have sex with each other.

Decide in advance whether either of you is free to date during the separation and under what circumstances. One couple who were continuing their separation after three months decided that it would be OK for each to kiss on dates and that light petting would be acceptable. Another couple decided that they would date but that they would not pick up partners in bars.

Decide whether engaging in sex with dates is acceptable and if so, under what circumstances. With the current concern about sexually transmitted diseases, this is important to discuss.

Try to experience really being separate. Stay out of each other's way. Don't follow each other around, don't third-degree each other about activities and whereabouts, and *don't* take your laundry home to be done even if you do it yourself.

### 7. After Everything Is Planned, Tell the Children.

Children need honesty and information during the divorce process. They also need time, sensitivity to their feelings, and confidence in their parents' ability to weather this crisis. As soon as you make the decision to separate and define the particulars, you need to decide how and what to tell the children. Children always remember, for the rest of their lives, how they were told of their parents' decision to separate or divorce. Considerable damage can be done if this task is done poorly.

Make sure you allow plenty of time. This is not a discussion that should be hurried through and no family member should have to rush off to do something else right after the discussion, especially either of the parents. Choose a time of day when there are no other distractions. Turn off the phone, TV, and radio, and tell the children you want to talk to them about something important. Do not tell the children separately. The entire family should sit down together to discuss this important event. It's best if both parents do some of the talking. But if one parent is too emotional to say much, at least both should be present.

Children do not need to hear any blame or veiled threats or hostile remarks. They should be told of the decision simply and honestly. Here's one way:

> Children, we have come to a very difficult decision and we wanted to tell you about it together and to give you time to ask us anything you might need to know. Daddy (Mommy) and I have decided to live apart for a while and be separated. We're not sure right now if it will be permanent. We might decide later on to get a divorce or we might be able to work out our problems and get back together again someday.
>
> For right now, we've decided to live apart for six months and then see how we feel. We're going to stay in therapy to work on our problems while we're separated.
>
> So, next week Daddy will be moving to his own apartment. There will be bedrooms and space there for all of you to stay with him some of the time. You'll be staying with him on Thursdays, Fridays, and Saturdays and with me the rest of the week. We'll separate some of the furniture and things in your rooms so you'll have toys and clothes and furniture there just like here. You'll be able to call either of us anytime you miss us and we'll be seeing each other pretty often to work on things.

You guys know that we've been pretty unhappy with each other for a long time. We've tried not to fight in front of you but you're all old enough to know it's been pretty awful lately and it's not fair to you for us to keep making everyone miserable.

It's important that you know that none of this is your fault. Nothing you did caused it and nothing you could have done would have changed it. Our problems are with each other, not with you, and we both love you very much.

You're not going to lose either of us, no matter what happens. But we need some time apart to figure out what we want and whether we can be happy with each other again. We want you to talk to either or both of us any time about this and ask any questions you need to, whenever you're worried about anything. We'll try to make plenty of time to talk to you.

At this point, children may have a variety of reactions. Some may shrug their shoulders and say, "OK. Can I go now?" Others may burst into tears and beg you not to do this. Others may be angry and yell at you, "How can you do this to us!"

Each child has an individual reaction depending on many factors. In any case, let all the children have whatever reaction they need to have. Tell them it's all right to be angry and sad, that these are normal feelings and are shared by everyone in the family. If children prefer not to react right away, let them have space and time to process what is happening. They may come around later to ask questions.

After telling the children about the separation, make sure you are available the rest of the day and in the days ahead. Talk to the children and answer their questions as carefully and fully as you can. They will have questions for many months to come but these first ones are critical to their eventual adjustment.

## PLANNING A HEALTHY PHYSICAL SEPARATION FOR YOUR CHILDREN

Your children are going to experience a lot of confusion and anxiety, and will probably flood you with questions you haven't even thought about yet. Here are some suggestions that will help you anticipate and plan for the needs of your children.

## Planning a Healthy Separation for the Children

1. Give them the gift of honesty.

2. Give them the gift of choice.

3. Give them the gift of patience and time.

4. Give them the gift of accurate information.

5. Give them the gift of trust.

6. Give them the gift of security and continuity.

7. Give them the gift of making them your highest priority.

### 1. Give Them the Gift of Honesty.

Be honest with your children about the reasons for the decision to separate, but try to refrain from blaming, criticizing, or exaggerating. Let their ages guide you in what to say and how much to say. Be calm and sensitive to their difficult position. You are asking them to accept a decision that they will probably see as unacceptable, a decision they have no control over, no power to change, and no ability to refuse.

### 2. Give Them the Gift of Choice.

Allow them their own individual reactions. Don't try to make them less sad or less mad. Don't try to align them with your position on the separation. Don't try to give them your anger or hurt or need for revenge.

### 3. Give Them the Gift of Patience and Time.

Answer all their questions openly, honestly, and as objectively as possible. Realize that they can process only pieces of your response at any given time and may feel compelled to ask the same thing again and again to process it from different angles and at different developmental levels. Try to be patient with this repetitive process.

### 4. Give Them the Gift of Accurate Information.

Try to give them information that will affect their eventual adjustment. Decide who will live where, in how big a place, in what school district. Decide on a predictable access plan and tell them about it right away. Talk to them about how they will get to school, who will help them with their homework, how they can stay in touch with their friends. If they are late teens, decide how college will be handled, if they plan to go to college. Also discuss other concerns, such as how to provide a car for their use. The more children know, the less they will be depressed and anxious and the faster they will adjust.

### 5. Give Them the Gift of Trust.

Don't lie in order to save their feelings. Don't give hope where there is no realistic hope or fuel their fantasies of life being no different after a separation. Children's sense of trust in their parents can be disrupted for a long time if lies or half truths are told during this crisis.

### 6. Give Them the Gift of Security and Continuity.

The process of selecting a second residence for one spouse to move into can be extremely important for children's eventual adjustment. Children manage this difficult transition better when they are involved in the process of change. It may be useful to take children with you to look at new places. Get their input about size, location, neighborhood facilities, and so on. Try to be sensitive to their needs and feelings while keeping a realistic eye on financial considerations.

Although it's not always a good idea for children to be present when the parent actually moves out, the timing of this move should not be a surprise. It *is* a good idea to have children help you move in and organize and decorate the new home. It is important to get their input about which toys, clothes, and furniture they would like to have at each home. If they are old enough, let them do some of their own packing.

Work with them to plan their new bedrooms and to create a cozy, warm atmosphere that will make them feel comfortable and wanted in your new place. Make sure all the children have some kind of space, bed, and drawers to call their own. If the space is small, create separate spaces with room dividers or creative placement of furniture. If money is a problem, shop for used furniture or unfinished furniture. Children will resist being in a home that feels cold, unfamiliar, and not kid-friendly.

### 7. Give Them the Gift of Making Them Your Highest Priority.

Try your best to put the children's needs above your own. Often what is best for the child is not what's best for the parent and vice versa. *Children's needs must be the higher priority.* They are the helpless victims of your choices and these choices may influence their adjustment for years to come. Decisions in divorce areas are among the most important decisions you may ever make regarding your children's well-being.

---

## STAGE 5
## PSEUDO-RECONCILIATION

For many couples, the experience of physical separation brings a sense of loss and apprehension after a few days or weeks. This may lead to what we call a *pseudoreconciliation.* Often people who have been married ten or fifteen years have rarely been by themselves and are not used to being alone. The first days of separation often trigger an uncomfortable sense of loneliness and a personal anguish about managing a household by themselves.

At this point, the earlier preseparation fantasies give way to a new range of feelings that the distancing spouses did not anticipate:

- A sense of loss when they are absent from their children

- Guilt over abandoning the family and their parental responsibilities

- Disapproval from their parents or other family members

- The continual emotional tugging by the spouse who is being left and the children. Even the children, as we'll see later, will create problems in an effort to get the separated parent back home.

The power of these feelings, particularly when considerable ambivalence still exists, can cause the former conflicts and unhappiness to appear minor. Thus the prospect of moving back in is often greeted with a sense of relief, a feeling of comfort in returning to a safe and secure place. Often the distancing parent who returns home is pampered with attention and gifts by the spouse and treated like a hero by the children. It can be like a second honeymoon.

But ending a separation prematurely can have mixed results. In some cases the new reality experienced during the separation can provide a window to reconsider the potential of the marriage. The distancing spouse may return to stage 1 and reexamine ambivalence. Both spouses may now be more motivated to seek marital therapy.

Unfortunately, however, ending the separation for reasons of loneliness and fear is not productive in most cases. The pseudoreconciliation simply covers up the original underlying dysfunctions. Often reuniting brings some superficial pleasure and contentment, but the reality remains under the surface. So the former pattern of conflicts begins to reemerge, sometimes slowly and often quickly.

We have worked with separated couples who reunited on a Friday night, had a big argument on Saturday, and were separated again by Sunday afternoon. Other couples may go through several cycles of getting back together and reseparating. One couple did this four times in three months.

This cycle of moving in and out is not healthy for you or your children! You can achieve a healthier separation if you:

- Identify and deal with the feelings that we have described in stages 1, 2, and 3.

- Plan with your partner the goals and ingredients of the separation as we have described above.

- Seek the help of a marital and family therapist before and during the separation.

## UNDERSTANDING YOUR CHILDREN'S FEELINGS

For children, a reconciliation is like a wish come true. They quickly jump to the conclusion that the separation was a bad dream from which they have awakened and which they can now forget. They try to deny the reemerging signs that all is not well as the attempt at reunion begins to fail. They often ask parents for reassurances that they are better or happier or still going to stay together, and cling to any superficial signs that things might be improving.

Unfortunately, this period of calm before returning storms leads to future difficulties for children in accepting the reality of divorce and will serve to make the disappointment of the subsequent separation more painful. For younger children, it will encourage their willingness to deny reality. They may think "If Mom and Dad got back together this time, they probably will again." This will make it harder for them to give up their fantasies of reconciliation even long after the divorce is past. Depression in children of all ages may be more likely after this period of pseudoreconciliation and a return of the stress and anxieties begins to be apparent.

When children are told again that the parents simply can't make the marriage work and are separating for the final time, many children experience considerable rage, even more intense than at the first separation. They feel duped and resent the parents for failing and letting them down. These intense reactions may be seen in a wide variety of moods and behaviors. If problematic emotional or physical responses occur and a healthier level does not return after a few weeks, you should consider seeing a child therapist to evaluate the need for short-term therapy to help the children through this crisis.

School behavior and performance are often very sensitive barometers of how children are feeling. If they take a nosedive, you need to pay attention, for they are important indicators of trouble. Take steps to assess the children's needs for professional assistance.

# 4

## The Decision to Divorce

FTER YOU HAVE PASSED THROUGH the various stages of ambivalence and distancing, the actual decision to divorce may not be quite as dramatic as you expected. Making this decision does represent, however, the most painful step in moving to end the marriage. To the extent that you can identify the issues and work on the tasks that we have suggested, this stage may be less unpredictable, less frightening, and therefore healthier for you and your children.

There is no question that the decision to divorce has far-reaching consequences for you and your family. Everyone has to give up the hope and fantasy of life returning to normal. Everyone may experience a sense of depression and anxiety related to the finality of this decision. Often, at this point, extended family and friends renew their efforts to get you and your spouse back together and alter your course toward divorce. However, by this time there is usually no turning back.

---

### STAGE 6
### PREDIVORCE FANTASIES

As you move through the physical separation it is likely that the underlying conflicts and disappointments will continue as before. If you have tried a reconciliation, then these old problems will simply resurface. This may take just a few days or several months, but when they do appear you will experience a greater sense of failure than you felt before. You may think: "I've tried everything and it's still the same." Or, "No matter what we do, we still can't make it work."

We call this stage *predivorce fantasies*. It's a time of gradual realization that divorce is inevitable and planning a course toward that final decision. The distancing spouse begins to plan for a separate life and may begin to talk about divorce more openly, perhaps for the first time, with friends and family members. Either spouse may begin to develop a budget, to save money, to consider new places to live, or to look for new job opportunities. Finally, the choice of a divorce mediator or attorney may begin the legal process. The fantasies at this stage are more down to earth and realistic than the fantasies of adventure and romance that we described in stages 1 through 3.

As you move closer to the decision to divorce, the balance within your family that we discussed in Chapter One may become further upset. The spouse who is not ready to let go may be feeling more anger, more rage, greater sadness, greater desperation. The children may be hurt and angry. Everyone may go through periods of both anxiety and depression. It is not likely that you and your spouse will make this final decision mutually. However, the more both of you have talked about this and proceeded through the stages we have discussed, and the more sufficient a passage of time, the better is your prospect of getting through this in a healthy manner.

For the children, moving toward this decision to divorce closes the door on hopes and fantasies that their family can return to a normal state again. This step may actually create relief in some children who are glad the ambiguity is over and they finally know what is to happen. For other children, those who prefer the ambiguity of hope to the finality of divorce, a new feeling of anxiety and desperation may emerge.

Many will beg or bargain. One six-year-old boy said to Craig at the conclusion of a family session where the parents had explained their plans for the divorce: "I'll give you everything in my piggy bank if you can make Daddy come back home." Others will begin to have vague physical complaints—headaches, stomachaches, or dizziness—to express their upset feelings. Some children will develop significant behavioral or academic problems or school phobias. Some may even attempt to run away from home. All these are desperate efforts to dissuade the parents from their course toward divorce and immature attempts to give their parents a common cause of concern in the hope that this might lead to another reconciliation.

A ten-year-old boy ran away from home (about three blocks away) the night before his parents' divorce hearing was scheduled. He said later, "I thought if they were worried and came to look for me they would get back together."

For the same reason, an eight-year-old girl faked acute stomach problems for three days at school and insisted that both parents accompany her to the physician's office. She imagined they would get back together again if they were worried about her.

Realize that these are all ways that children are attempting to adjust to a frightening and unwanted family situation. With sufficient time, patience, and love, these difficulties will pass and the children begin to return to a more settled and adjusted place.

---

## STAGE 7
## THE DECISION
## TO DIVORCE

The decision to divorce represents the central turning point in this continuum we call the divorce process. The probability of turning back now drastically diminishes. The sense of finality can be deadening to the spouse who is being left, while producing a sense of relief to the spouse who is leaving.

Up until this point, both partners were still examining the relationship and considering potential ways of repairing it. Even the distancing spouse hung on to some threads of hope. In the previous six stages couples dealt with the interplay of ambivalence and distancing and with the potential for reconciliation. There was the experience of movement, interaction, loyalties, and even a sense of protection for each other and the family. Now this dance of pushing, pulling, hoping, and giving up comes to an end.

The most notable change that occurs here, and the most disruptive to achieving a healthy divorce, is the loss of an underlying sense of protectiveness between the spouses. Therapists call this a collusive bond. All relationships that endure the first couple of years together develop this underlying and usually unspoken bond. It's a kind of quid pro quo—if you protect my sensitive places, I will protect yours; I won't tell on you, if you don't tell on me.

All spouses know intuitively the most sensitive and vulnerable parts of their partner. They know which buttons to push if they want to cause hurt. They also know how far to go and where to stop when arguments escalate. These are the boundaries of the collusive or protective bond.

Even in the most conflicted relationships this bond usually remains intact. Sometimes when one spouse is hurt badly by the other, such as by an affair, he or she will retaliate by threatening this bond. But the decision to divorce is about the only event in a couple's life that can end this bond. When the decision is made, the dance is over. Spouses will say:

"I never thought you would let it come to this."

"I never believed you could do this to me and the children."

"I feel betrayed and lonely."

"You can't be the same person I loved."

"You are my whole life. How could you do this?"

"I don't even know who you are any more."

Of course, divorce does not have to destroy this bond. In fact, preserving some of it is an essential ingredient of a healthy divorce and continued co-parenting. We have seen many couples who still feel supportive and protective of their former spouses five or ten years after their divorces, even though they have remarried and built new lives.

But when the decision to divorce is made, this bond is clearly threatened. The first assault often comes from the spouse who is left. The sense of rejection turns to anger and vengeance. Threats are made, money is taken from joint accounts, the other spouse's relationship with the children and even extended family is sabotaged or threatened. Often attorneys are brought into the picture at this point, which adds another level to the threats and accusations. This also creates more pressure to break this bond as attorneys gear up to do battle and gather ammunition for the fight (we will discuss this further in Chapter Six).

If you are the spouse who is leaving, you may have never expected the intensity of your partner's anger and retaliations. Try to remember that underneath all this, however, are intense hurt and feelings of abandonment, rejection, loss, and grief. This is why it is so important for divorcing couples to talk about all these feelings during the earlier six stages.

This unexpected reaction by a spouse was demonstrated when Craig was asked to consult on a case with a psychiatrist colleague. After years of conflict and unhappiness in their marriage, the wife had contacted an attorney and told the husband the marriage was over. The husband reacted by threatening to kill his wife and children and then himself, and had been immediately hospitalized. His wife proceeded with filing, and divorce papers were served on the husband in the hospital.

Holding the papers, the husband sobbed uncontrollably. "I never thought she would actually divorce me. She and the children were all I had. I worked hard all my life for them. She betrays me now that I'm close to retirement." He saw no reason to go on living.

The husband denied that he had meant any harm toward his wife or children, but several guns were found and no one can know if he would have hurt them in a moment of rage. Fortunately, during the hospitalization he was able to look past the marriage and identify some new directions for himself. It took him nearly a year to repair the relationships with his children that were damaged by his reactions to the divorce.

The breakdown of this protective bond can also be seen clearly when divorcing parents get into custody fights over their children. We mentioned earlier that we have been involved with hundreds of custody evaluations for attorneys and the courts. Often the ugliest side of the divorce process emerges here. The legal system, which we will discuss in the next chapter, unwittingly provides the arena that pits parent against parent. To the victor go the children—but often with irreparable damage to all.

The implicit rules of surviving a fight over the custody of your children dictate that the former protective bond between you and your partner must be set aside. You are on your own. You may want to make your spouse look as bad and as dangerous as possible while at the same time protecting your own image as a parent. It is an unpleasant and destructive process that damages both parents and children.

Old issues that were never mentioned during the marriage may now be made public by your partner. Some people even make charges that they know are either exaggerated or even totally false. Suddenly you may find the same kind of accusations coming out of your mouth:

Suspected affairs, now or years ago

Having an abortion in the past

Abusive behavior toward the children, such as hitting your son with a belt or pulling your daughter's hair

Charges of incest

Impotency

Suspected homosexuality

Frigidity

Sexual perversions such as cross-dressing or wearing opposite-sex underwear

Stealing at work

Alcoholic or abusive parents

Alleged sexual molestation of your child

The last item on our list above represents the epitome of the breakdown of the protective bond between a couple. This allegation of molestation has become so common in custody disputes over the past decade that a whole collection of books and articles has been written to help professionals understand and deal with it. A prominent child psychiatrist, Dr. Richard Gardner, has even developed an extensive checklist to help professionals try to determine whether a child was indeed molested or whether it was a fabrication by the other parent. (See Appendix for other books by Dr. Gardner.) This is perhaps the ultimate charge, and it will debase and cloud the image of a parent for the rest of his or her life.

We worked over a period of nine months with a divorcing couple who disagreed on their five-year-old daughter's visitation plan. We were asked to attempt to mediate a custody and access agreement or, if a mutual agreement could not be reached, to complete a custody evaluation with specific recommendations about the type of custody and amount of time the daughter would spend with each parent.

We quickly discovered that the couple had great difficulty communicating without fighting and threatening one another. The wife was very angry at her husband for leaving her, and felt that she deserved more control over her daughter Sarah. However, the father's job allowed him flexible time and he had been Sarah's primary caretaker during most of her life. The mother also was prone to intense outbursts and threats. Often she would lose patience with Sarah and become physical. She became so frustrated with Sarah during an interview with Sandy that she would not continue and another session had to be scheduled.

It was not possible to help them reach an agreement so we completed our evaluation. During this period neither parent expressed concerns or made charges about the other parent with regard to alcohol, drug abuse, violence, or sexual abuse. We always ask parents individually about these areas.

In our final report we stated that we felt both parents could be effective with their child, particularly after the animosity of the divorce had settled. We recommended slightly more time with the father because he was more comfortable in his parenting and Sarah was more bonded to him.

The day after the attorneys and parents received our report, the mother contacted Child Protective Services and stated that she had suspected for a long time that her husband had been sexually molesting her daughter. There had never been any mention of this earlier, and our time with Sarah had indicated that the only harm she had experienced was the trauma of being pulled into the middle of the divorce. This was a sad and desperate attempt by the mother to get back at her husband. Eventually the court awarded sole custody to the father and required that the mother begin therapy to help her accept the court's decision.

## TELLING YOUR CHILD ABOUT
## YOUR FINAL DECISION

Many of the guidelines for telling your children of your separation (see Chapter Three) also apply when you tell them of the decision to divorce. Both of you need to meet with the children together. Try to tell them calmly, clearly, and simply. "We have tried everything we know of and we haven't been able to make our marriage work well enough to get back together again. So we've decided to get a divorce."

At this point, it's important to give the children whatever information you can about how this process will work. If you have already been separated for some time, this decision will not come as any surprise to them. They may have been preparing themselves emotionally for a long time. If this is the case, they may have a very minimal reaction to the news. It may also be true for them that very little will change from the separation to the divorce. It is a legal procedure that, in practical terms, is of far more significance for the adults than the children. Often, the parents continue the same routines and arrangements they had designed for the separation period after the divorce. (There is considerable benefit to the children in doing so, incidentally.)

For many children, therefore, the actual divorce is a confusing abstraction that doesn't change their life very much. Many young children think of the separation as the divorce because that is where their grieving process began. One child told us, "I don't know what the big deal is—seems like they got divorced a long time ago."

Depending on the age of the child, the main concerns about divorce are:

Who will take care of me?

How will I be able to be with both of you?

Will my mom or dad be all right?

Will I still have all the things I'm used to around me?

The older the child, the greater is the understanding of the significance of the event. Older children worry about whether there will still be a car for them to use or whether they'll still be able to go to college. One of the biggest questions for older children is, "Will Mom or Dad get married again and make me live with some stranger?"

Younger children are often anxious for parents to find a new partner. In fact, frequently, they act as recruiters for their parents, propositioning each possible prospect about whether they'd like to be their new mommy or daddy. These questions can provide some of life's more embarrassing moments! Older children are much more negative about their parent's dating and possible remarriage. We'll discuss this issue at greater length later.

Some children, however, do react to this final divorce decision very strongly, even if you have been separated for some time. As a general rule, the greater the denial the child has built up, the greater will be the reaction to the announcement. Some children will cry uncontrollably, some will plead and beg for you to change your mind, others may become extremely angry and scream at you for being "dumb and stupid" and say they will "hate you forever" if you go through with your decision. There are many variations but essentially they reflect children's fear of the unknown, anxiety about the future, and anger that they are helpless to dissuade you.

Children are powerless in this process toward divorce. They don't have veto power over their parents' decision and typically cannot, through any means, get their parents back together again. By this time they may have attempted many things.

- They may have tried to strike a bargain with you: "I'll keep my room clean all the time and get straight A's if you'll get back together again."

- They may have tried guilt: "How can you do this to me? You don't love me at all!"

- They may have tried threats: "I'll run away if you get a divorce" or "I would rather be dead than for you to get a divorce."

- They may have tried worrying you, by eating much less or having some mysterious illness or letting their grades plummet.

- They may have pleaded, begged, yelled, or been depressed—and all to no avail because divorces rarely are caused by children.

Frustrated, frightened, and hopeless, children may grasp at straws in desperate last-minute attempts to change the inevitable course toward divorce.

What can you do about these reactions? Accept them. Be sensitive to the feelings they portray. Continue to be loving and allow your children to process their own responses. Appreciate how they are feeling. Say something like this:

> You have every right to be angry (or sad) and it's OK to let me know how you feel. I know you're hurt and upset and it's OK to tell me all of your feelings. I can't change this decision. I hope you'll be able to understand and forgive us someday. Meanwhile, we'll both be here for you to talk to if you're scared or mad or sad or whatever you're feeling. And we believe things will begin to feel better soon when all these changes are behind us. We both love you and will be there for you if you need us for anything.

Often all children need to get past this difficult stage is reassurance that all will be better and security that they will not lose either parent.

## PROTECTING YOUR CHILD IN THE MIDST OF THE DIVORCE

It has been our experience over twenty years of working with divorcing couples that with very few exceptions parents want to do what's best for their children. No matter what are the particulars of the divorce, however hostile or messy, parents love their children and want to protect them from harm. Unfortunately, it is very difficult for some parents to actually *do* what is best for their children during a divorce. Their own feelings, needs, hurts, disappointments, fears, and anxieties cloud and impair their judgment. Oftentimes, divorcing couples don't really know what is best for their children and therefore behave in ways that can be truly damaging and destructive.

Once again: What is best for the parents is often the opposite of what is best for the children. At the very height of confusion and pain, parents are asked to ignore their own needs to take care of their children's needs and feelings. This requires an incredible amount of maturity and responsibility. Unfortunately many parents cannot manage all this when they're at such a low point emotionally.

The more you can recognize the need to protect the children, however, the more quickly they'll be able to make a healthy adjustment. Here are some suggestions:

1. Don't demean or speak harshly of your spouse to or around the children. Don't allow anyone else to do so.

2. Don't use the children as barter in your divorce negotiations. Don't say "You can have an extra day with the children if you increase your child support $100 per month" or "You can keep the house if I can have joint custody."

3. Develop an access system that allows for frequent and relatively equal time with the children. Develop a predictable, consistent schedule that has the potential for occasional flexibility.

4. Encourage your children to express their feelings (negative *and* positive) freely, openly, and without any form of judgment or criticism from you.

5. Encourage a loving, supportive, quality relationship with the other parent.

6. Always make time to answer children's questions about divorce-related issues. Never lie but always consider the children's ages and feelings in your response and in how much detail you give.

7. Don't pretend about your own feelings and don't try to give your feelings to your children. It's all right to say "I'm very angry with your father" but important to add "but that doesn't mean you need to be angry with him."

8. Do not use your children to communicate with or spy on the other parent. Don't say, "Tell your father to stop calling me so much" or "Tell me all about Mom's new boyfriend." Don't interrogate your children about the details of the other parent's life or home. If they volunteer information, be pleasant and enthusiastic but don't ask for other details. If a child reports, "Guess what, Daddy has a new girlfriend," don't say, "Oh really? What does she look like? How long has he known her? Does she stay overnight with him?" The correct response is "Oh really? That's nice. Did you have fun this weekend?"

9. Be *very* careful how you handle your feelings about a new love interest of your former spouse's. This person may someday be a

stepparent for your children, and what you say may cause him or her significant difficulties later on. Don't refer to "that bitch" or "that jerk." Try to stay neutral if you can't be positive. Work with a therapist if your feelings are too severe. Don't burden your children so that in order to prove they love you they have to hate the new person in Mom's or Dad's life.

## STAGE 8
## EXPERIENCING
## AMBIVALENCE

Even as couples proceed this far into the divorce process and believe that they have made a final decision to end the relationship, an amazing feeling of ambivalence can resurface. In Chapter One we saw ambivalence as a gauge of your relative attachment and commitment to the marriage. And in Chapter Three we saw that often loneliness can trigger thoughts of reconciliation. Stage 8 represents a period of cold feet, when you may question whether you really should pursue the divorce. It is similar to the questioning we described in stage 5 (pseudoreconciliation), but now based on the heavy dose of reality from attorneys and the legal procedures that invade your life during this later stage of divorce.

In addition to the legal realities, now the levels of anger and animosity and the threats over children and money can create a sense of being overwhelmed, of wondering—"Is this really worth it?" The destruction of the protective bond between you and your partner often creates a sense of loss or melancholy. Confusing feelings of ambivalence emerge and you long for memories of quiet family vacations. You may even feel nostalgic for the struggle and conflict that existed between you just a few months ago.

When working with couples at this stage we consider two possible directions:

1. Does this reappearance of ambivalence and thoughts of reconciliation offer a genuine "therapeutic window" for the couple to return to working on repairing their marriage? We are very careful here not to give couples false hope, but we also don't want to

miss a last potential opportunity to help them preserve their relationship.

2. Does this stage simply represent one or both spouses' feeling overwhelmed by the intensity, intrusions, and complexities of this decision to divorce and the legal path that lies ahead?

In the majority of cases this second direction is what people are experiencing. Usually they simply need to slow down the divorce process. Sometimes we encourage spouses to meet and interact with each other, often with their therapist present, to bypass the intrusive role of the attorneys. The goal is to be clear about their concerns and proceed in a more objective and healthier manner.

As we said in the pseudoreconciliation stage, allowing yourself to be pulled back into the marriage for reasons of fear, intimidation, or confusion will not provide magical or productive outcomes. If you are tempted to do this, talk out your feelings with your therapist first.

We worked with a couple who had been married ten years and had two young sons. Their divorce issues had become adversarial and the attorneys asked us to help them mediate a suitable resolution. The primary dispute involved the wife's decision to relocate to California where her parents and siblings lived. They had agreed to joint custody but the husband would not accept her moving. At first he attempted to make her feel guilty. Then he turned to threats of proving her a bad mother. She became depressed and overwhelmed by this but continued her resolve to leave the marriage for her own health.

After an access plan was proposed that would allow the father considerable time with the children and other financial issues were settled, he accepted the children's move to California. But on the morning before they were to leave for California, the mother called and asked for an emergency appointment. Her ambivalence and uncertainty had resurfaced. She had many questions:

"Do you really think I am doing the right thing?"

"Do you think their father will abandon them?"

"Do you think I should have just been satisfied with what I had?"

"Do you think I will ever feel like even talking to a man again?"

"Do you think my family will accept me now that I'm divorced?"

"Do you think I will ever get over this?"

If you are experiencing this stage of doubt and recurring ambivalence, be very careful to protect your children from further confusion and anxiety by *not* sharing your doubts and questions with them. It may only strengthen their denial about the reality of the divorce and reignite their wish for reconciliation.

The more doubts you share, the greater may be their resolve to play on them and believe what they want to believe. Knowing about your doubts can also increase children's anger toward the spouse who is less ambivalent. They may see the distancing parent as the one who wants to break up the family and the more doubtful parent as wanting to keep the family together. This forces an alignment that can be detrimental for the children and for their relationship with the distancing spouse.

Sometimes this sharing of doubts and fears is done deliberately to get the children on one spouse's side and to pressure the other spouse into returning to the family home and marriage. Some parents don't actually *want* their children to accept and adjust to the divorce because of their own inability to do so. But it is not healthy for your children to cling to this fantasy of reuniting because it can leave them depressed and anxious for many years.

As one eight-year-old told Sandy, "I used to cry myself to sleep wishing my parents would live together again. But now I guess I can see where everyone is a lot happier than they used to be and maybe it's not so bad after all."

# 5

## Ending the Dance: The Decisions You Must Make in the Divorce

**Y**OU HAVE MADE THE DECISION to divorce, and soon you will be involved in a legal action, either adversarial or mediated. That is the subject of the next chapter. For now, we want to help you to think about what is actually involved in this divorce experience.

There are many choices and decisions to be made over the next few months, choices that will affect you and your children for years to come. We want you to be informed about the practical concerns so you won't be surprised or overwhelmed when an attorney or mediator confronts you with these issues.

The more you can understand what's ahead, the more you will feel in control of the decisions, the more likely you and your spouse will be able to achieve a healthy divorce.

We can't emphasize this too much: *Educate yourself* about what is ahead!

Let's begin with an extensive list of specific issues about which you and your spouse will have to decide. We won't discuss all of these here, since many will be covered in the next chapter. There are also books in our suggested reading list (Appendix A) to help you. Think of these as a preliminary checklist, like the one an airline pilot reviews before takeoff to ensure a "safe" flight. The more you and your spouse can discuss these issues together, the better you'll be prepared for the actual divorce.

## The Divorce Decision-Making List

### CUSTODY AND ACCESS ISSUES

1. Legal custody: joint, sole, divided, or split

2. Physical custody: shared, sole, split, or alternating

3. Access during the school year

4. Access during the summers

5. Transportation between households

6. Telephone contact during residential and travel periods

7. Holiday access plan

8. Access to grandparents and extended family members

9. Travel out of the city or state

10. Annual review of access plan

11. Negotiation or mediation when major life events occur

12. Child support: formulas and guidelines

13. Health and dental care for children: insurance and sharing costs not covered by insurance

14. Choice of school or day care and after-school care or activities

15. Handling religious education

The list can help you begin to consider the many areas you'll be asked to make decisions about. Also, books in the Appendix offer considerable detail, particularly in the areas of financial, property, and tax matters: *The Divorce Decisions Workbook* by Marjorie Engel and Diana Gould, and *Divorce Yourself: The National No-Fault Divorce Kit* by Daniel Sitarz.

16. Setting up a college fund: whether or not and how to

17. Continuing or beginning lessons for children: who and how to pay

18. Remedial help and necessary tutoring for the children: who and how to pay

19. Costs of day care or after-school care

FINANCIAL AND PROPERTY ISSUES

20. Spousal maintenance: alimony

21. To sell the house or not

22. Division of financial assets: savings, investments, pension and other retirement plans

23. Division of personal property: from pots and pans to furniture and automobiles

24. Division of debts: charge accounts, mortgage, loans

25. The need for appraisals of property or business interests

26. Changing bank accounts and credit cards

27. Tax issues: claiming a child, support, alimony, inheritances

## UNDERSTANDING YOUR CHOICES IN CHILD CUSTODY

Parents are often confused about what the different child custody arrangements really mean. So we'll try to define several models and give a perspective so you can make the best choices for you and your children.

## TYPES OF CUSTODY ARRANGEMENTS

*Joint custody* is now recognized in most states and in many jurisdictions is favored or mandated by the court. So if you live in one of those states and you *don't* want joint custody, one or both parents must object and convince the court that it won't work.

Joint custody is simply the definition that both parents will continue in the eyes of the law as equal partners in the process of raising the children, just as when they were married. Joint custody does not define how much time the children spend with each parent.

But it can become more complicated than this. In most states there are independent definitions of joint legal and joint physical custody.

*Joint legal custody* means that both parents will have the right to share in the major decisions that will affect their children's lives. This involves education, health and medical issues, religious preferences, and their social environment. Of course these decisions *must be made jointly.* When parents cannot agree or negotiate such choices, there are usually provisions in the final divorce agreement that spell out how such disagreements will be handled. For example, disputes in this area could be negotiated by a mediator or counselor, or one parent could be specified as making the final decision.

*Joint physical custody* has several variations. *Primary physical custody* designates who the children will live with the majority of the time and which parent will make the everyday decisions for the children on such things as haircuts, dental appointments, and dance lessons. In some states this is more accurately termed *primary physical residence.* It may seem something of a contradiction to award parents joint legal custody and then turn around and define one parent as physical custodian. This policy stems from the courts' and legislatures' concern for protecting the stability of the family and household environment, particularly for young children. Some states will enforce the definition of physical custody more than others.

But things can get even more complicated because the physical custody may also be defined as shared, split, or alternating.

*Shared physical custody* means parents have the children with them approximately half the time. In this designation, neither parent is presumed to have any sole decision-making power. Day-to-day decisions are made by whoever is the residential parent when the situation arises.

This type of custody requires a great deal of communication and cooperation between parents, who must be fairly adept at solving conflict and resolving disputes. It also helps if they have similar styles of parenting and similar values about raising their children.

*Split physical custody* means that both parents are awarded physical custody at separate but specific times of the year. An example would be physical custody with the father from January through June and with the mother from July through December. A more common pattern is physical custody with one parent during the school year and the other parent during the summers. Thus, if the children live with the father during the school year in Virginia, physical custody would be with him for that period and then with the mother in California during the summers.

*Alternating physical custody* is very similar and in some states would not be seen as different from split physical custody. It means that physical custody would be defined as alternating between the parents in some predetermined and consistent way. In states where physical custody must be designated separately from joint custody, it could simply mean that the parent with whom the children are in residence is defined as having physical custody.

While these two categories may be confusing, they are usually employed for technical reasons in a legal context to achieve or define equal or balanced power in a divorce settlement. Try not to be confused here; in most cases these designations do not really define the access plan or where the children are living at a given time.

*Sole custody* was the traditional model of custody for many decades, based on an early, somewhat uninformed belief that children need the security and stability of staying in one place. It means that only *one parent* is awarded the legal *and* physical custody of the children. This parent has *complete control* of all decisions about child rearing. The noncustodial parent has no legal rights with the children except the designated time to visit. In many states the noncustodial parent will not be allowed to see school or medical records for their children and cannot even sign for their child's medical treatment without a written consent document from the custodial parent.

You need to know that many traditionally trained judges, attorneys, and therapists still favor this model.

## WHAT IS BEST?

Before the first half of this century, all custody decisions went to the father because children were considered property and males were the holders of the property in families. Later rulings for sole custody in courts across the country almost always favored the mother. In many states fathers were not considered eligible for custody even if the mothers had a history of neglect and abuse. It was not until therapists, researchers, and eventually fathers' advocate groups questioned traditional beliefs that the model of joint custody became more acceptable.

Sole custody is very narrow and restrictive. It should not be used as a means of getting revenge or control over your spouse. Never lose sight of this vital question: What's in the best interest of your children?

Sole custody *is* a reasonable choice where one parent has historically demonstrated a lack of interest or ability to parent responsibly. Also, a career-oriented parent who expects to travel excessively may agree that the other parent should have sole custody. Sole custody is often indicated where one parent has a history of abuse toward the children, has problems with alcohol, drugs, or other substance abuse, or has psychiatric or medical conditions that would limit or impair the ability to parent responsibly. On occasions where either parent has severe difficulties in any of these areas, access with the children may need to be supervised by the court or a community agency.

Sole custody is not necessarily indicated if your wife had an affair with your best friend last year and you want to teach her a lesson, or if your husband smoked marijuana in high school ten years ago, or if you can't agree on whose religious preference the children should follow. Sole custody may not be beneficial to your children unless they need to be protected!

After several decades of experience with custody models around the country, many studies now show that joint custody offers the healthiest postdivorce adjustment for your children. There are three primary reasons for this.

First, both parents experience themselves as complete and involved parents with equal co-parenting responsibilities and opportunities. Children sense when a parent has second-class status and no official authority over issues related to them. Research has also shown (in this case with a comparison of joint custodial and noncustodial fathers) that financial responsibilities are met more consistently with the joint custodial fathers and that returning to court over child-related issues is reduced in joint-custody families.

Second, research also shows that the one greatest factor in children's adjustment to their parent's divorce is that they have frequent and regular contact with both parents. Please read one of the following books (see Appendix): *Surviving the Breakup: How Children and Parents Cope with Divorce* by Judith Wallerstein and Joan Kelly, or *Second Chances: Men, Women and Children a Decade After Divorce* by Wallerstein and Sandra Blakeslee.

Finally, joint custody tends to reduce the level of hostility and animosity that can persist after court battles over sole custody or property issues. The second most important factor for children's healthy adjustment after divorce is how quickly the parents are able to give up their anger and hostility and begin to co-parent effectively. The longer it takes, the greater the level of postdivorce adjustment problems for the children.

We strongly favor joint custody for most families, except for the situations noted above. In fact, to help achieve a healthy divorce, we recommend that you educate yourself about the values and patterns of joint custody for the benefit of both your own parenting and the needs and development of your children. And we hope you'll read some of the books related to joint custody that we list in the Appendix.

## PLANNING ACCESS

Access, or visitation, represents how you define the time your children will spend with each parent. We prefer the word *access* over *visitation*, which implies that they are "just visiting" in the other parent's household. Visitation is a somewhat outmoded concept related to sole custody where the children did in fact "only visit" the other parent.

Remember, the access plan that you and your spouse develop is not necessarily tied to the type of custody arrangement. For example, some parents may agree to a sole custody model but the children may spend almost equal time in both households. Or the parents may have joint custody but the children live most of the year with a parent in Texas and only see the other parent in Connecticut for a few weeks in the summers.

The most important thing is to decide what type of plan makes sense for the needs and style of your family. Some states have published access or visitation guidelines. These are often based on the ages of the children and are usually an attempt to define only the minimal times children should spend "visiting" the other parent. They are intended to assist the court and attorneys when serious disputes arise between parents. In most cases, if you and your spouse agree on a model the court will accept it as long as you can show it represents the best interests of your children.

No matter what ages your children are, you may want to consult with a child or family therapist who has experience working in the

## The Access Planning List

1. The age of each child: infant to two, three to five, six to ten, eleven to fourteen, fifteen to eighteen

2. Their closeness and attachment to each other

3. Their closeness and attachment to each parent

4. How they are handling the separation and divorce

5. The residences of each parent: how far apart, size, and adequacy

6. The location of school districts and the quality of education

7. The difficulties in changing schools

8. The need for day care or babysitting

9. The need for after-school care or activities

10. Transportation from each residence to the schools

11. The work and travel schedule of the father

12. The work and travel schedule of the mother

13. The availability of backup babysitting for each parent

divorce area. The therapist can help you develop an access plan that will take into consideration the developmental stages of your children, their adjustment needs, and the circumstances of both parents. The Access Planning List in this section summarizes practical considerations for planning an effective access model.

The access pattern you develop can have a great deal to do with your children's healthy adjustment to the divorce. *Do not bargain access issues with financial and support matters.* Most state courts have upheld the concept that access and support issues are not related in any way. For example, one parent may be ordered to pay child support but have no access to the children at all.

Also, don't expect attorneys or judges to be experts on child development or the emotional issues related to access plans. Step back, get professional assistance if you and your spouse can't talk about this easily, and plan a realistic schedule for the benefit of your children. Review the model access plan in Appendix C.

## CUSTODY AND ACCESS ISSUES FOR CHILDREN

It's important to understand that while children's needs and feelings must be strongly considered in custody and access decisions, the parents must be the decision makers, not the children! Children past the age of twelve or thirteen are often able to offer greater input and will typically let parents know their preference on both issues. This is also about the age where the courts will consider children's stated preferences. However, even at this age we discourage the role of children in such decisions, particularly where they have been pressured into alliances with one parent against another.

If your children are younger than twelve, you can do damage if you give them the impression that these decisions are up to them. It's even more damaging to actually give them the power to make these extremely difficult and significant decisions. *Children should not be expected or asked to choose between their parents, or to make value judgments about their parents' fitness or ability to properly parent.* The guilt that can follow from being forced into this position by parents who are abdicating their own responsibility can follow children throughout the rest of their lives.

In making these decisions for your children you need to consider their need for regular, meaningful, ongoing contact with *both* parents, for continuity, stability, security, predictability, and structure—albeit with some flexibility. It's a tall order but it can be done. If both parents can set aside their own hurts and disappointments and plan for their children's futures together, the children will greatly benefit.

Custody issues are fairly abstract and complicated, particularly for young children. They typically see custody as "who I'm going to live with." Custody is far more an issue for parents. It establishes rules and boundaries around power and control over the children, sometimes with considerable financial repercussions. The adversarial nature of divorce disputes seems to evoke more threats, animosity, and anger around issues of custody than access. Yet for most families, the access decisions have many more far-reaching consequences for children than custody decisions. How access is arranged can give structure, stability, predictability, and security. Access can be developed so that each parent maintains a very meaningful relationship with all their children.

Unfortunately, the courts and attorneys in many states have been very slow to incorporate what we know from research and clinical experience to be the best ways to plan an access model. Many courts and attorneys continue to promote access guidelines that are often too minimal for one parent (often the father) to maintain or develop a meaningful relationship with the children. As we discuss in the next chapter, the more you can work out your own custody and access determinations and avoid the adversarial system, the more you'll be able to build in greater variations. And this kind of flexibility will benefit you and your children in achieving a healthier divorce.

Although each family's situation needs to be considered individually, here are some general guidelines for considering these issues of access.

- The younger the child, the greater the need for frequent contact with both parents, particularly with the less available parent. The length or duration of contact, however, is less important. Infants and very young children need frequent contact because they don't have years of memories to rely on during times of no contact. Their knowledge of the parents needs to be frequently replenished to keep that parent familiar and continue the psychological bond. Even a couple of hours three times a week will help to keep the parent's image fresh and comfortable for the infant. Duration of time can be increased as the child matures. If both parents have participated almost equally in the basic caretaking of the child from birth, then the duration of visits can be longer.

- As children mature beyond preschool age, duration becomes more important than frequency for the quality of the relationship with the less available parent. From the age of three or so, the lengths of visits and inclusion of overnights become more important. The child should be comfortable with the parent at this point. The longer duration of a visit assists with promoting a sense of security and stability with both parents. Very short visits begin to feel too brief and can be somewhat disruptive to children as they become older.

- If you are considering a type of access that is distributed evenly (about fifty-fifty) our experience is that there are two choices that seem to work best. For children from about three to about six or seven, splitting the week in half is the best choice because young children need more frequent contact with each parent. If they go longer than three or four days they begin to worry about where the other parent is. For children from six or seven to about thirteen, alternating entire weeks can work well.

  Alternating segments longer than one week has drawbacks because the children begin to miss the other parent and planning activities with friends can become confusing. Alternating segments less than half weeks also has drawbacks, the most significant being the sense of bouncing back and forth. Some children can tolerate the frequent changes easily, others have a lot of trouble with it.

- Try, if parents' work schedules permit, to include both weekend time and weekday time for each parent with the children. Many difficulties for parents and children can be avoided if this is done. The traditional division of weekday time to the custodial parent and weekend time to the other parent has created a great many problems for families. It encourages one parent to be the ogre who has to discipline the children and provide structure and consistency, while the other parent becomes the playmate who can do all the fun things. The ideal for children is when both parents share discipline, provide structure, help with homework, and also go with the children to fun places where they can be carefree and spontaneous.

We have worked with literally hundreds of children who were living in separated and divorced homes with a wide variety of access patterns. We hope you will try to be creative and not see only one rigid or restrictive pattern for your children.

- The issue most consistently shared with us by the greatest majority of children from ages five through fourteen is that they want a pattern that feels fair to both parents. They are often angry if they think one parent was shortchanged. They feel sorry for this parent. They may also think the other parent is being cruel or unfair. This often becomes a factor in children's deciding that they want a change of custody when they become teenagers; they want to balance the score a bit and give the other parent a chance.

  A vengeful attitude that created an unequal access settlement may come back to haunt parents when angry adolescents confront them with having limited or ruined their relationship with their other parent. They may accuse one parent of having kept them from really knowing a father or a mother. This anger can damage the relationship with the overcontrolling parent for many years. So think through these decisions very carefully!

- It is our experience that most access patterns can work well with children as long as the guidelines we have mentioned have been taken into account. Ultimately, the most important consideration is the attitude of both parents toward the plan chosen. If both are enthusiastic and supportive, if both do their best to be consistent and reliable in making it work properly and predictably, and if both feel that it is truly in the best interest of the children, then most plans will work very well.

- Realize that all plans will need reworking and modifications as children grow up and families change. A built-in annual review is essential to allow for adjustments and fine tuning.

## WHY SOME ACCESS PLANS MAY FAIL

There are other factors to be aware of in developing access plans for children. Many parents complain that the plan itself is at fault when, in fact, not considering these other factors has been the primary cause of failure.

Any plan may fail if the two homes in which the children will be residing are quite unequal. Children often resist going to be with a parent who has not set up a child-sensitive environment. Children need to feel wanted. They need special areas for them in both homes. If a parent doesn't make an attempt to create a cozy, warm atmosphere where they have their own bed and drawers and space for toys and hobbies, then the children will prefer to be at the home where they do feel welcome and planned for.

When you separate, divide the children's clothes and toys and some of their furniture, sheets, posters, and so on so that the new place has a feel of home and some familiar surroundings. Children don't want to pack a suitcase every time they change homes. Have all their usual needs available to them in each home as soon as possible. A favorite blanket or stuffed animal may need to go back and forth, but try to make each home equally pleasant and fun.

Many children tell us that one reason they don't want to go to the other parent's house is that it's boring. Although this is often the tip of the iceberg in terms of what's really wrong, they complain that there's nothing to play with, nothing to eat, no place of their own to sleep, and that the parent makes no effort to be with them, play with them, or involve them in his or her everyday life.

Unfortunately, these complaints are most commonly made about single fathers. Sometimes, fathers may need to make greater efforts to get to know their children and to develop better parenting skills when they are first separated or divorced. If they are deficient in these areas, children will begin to resist being with the father. If you have not been very active as a father before the divorce, seek out men's groups, parent skills classes or workshops, and other single dads for advice in these areas. You'll reap great benefits in the quality of your relationships and your children will be far happier and healthier as a result of your efforts.

Another factor that will impair any access plan is the continued fighting or animosity between parents. When children are caught in the conflict between parents and quizzed when they arrive at each residence about what the other parent is doing, they'll resist spending time with that parent. (We will discuss how to make access plans work better in Chapter Seven.)

One common flaw that we see in many access plans is that they're too complicated or confusing for both parents and children. We helped one family revise their access plan a year after their divorce. The children had actually rebelled because it was so complicated: they had to switch residences four times in seven days. The access plan needs to be clear, sensible, and structured for the benefit of the children, not just the parents. If children do change residences several times a week, we often recommend that parents keep a calendar in each residence and color code the days in each household. This is particularly useful for young children.

## CHILDREN'S THOUGHTS ON CUSTODY AND ACCESS
The following quotes from children caught in custody battles demonstrate the power of these issues.

*Mark, age eight*

"I don't think either one of them should get me. All they ever do is fight and yell at each other. I'd rather live with my grandma."

*Susan, age twelve*

"They always made loving them feel like a contest, with one a loser and one a winner. I just want to love them both. Why can't they just stop making me feel guilty every time I have a good time with the other one?"

*David, age five*

"Dad says he wants me there but every time we go over all he does is watch football and drink beer. I don't think he really wants us. I think he just says that to make Mommy mad."

*Mary, age ten*

"I hate going to my dad's because every time I come back I get the third degree from Mom about what we did and who was there and whether Dad did anything wrong or anything that made us mad. I feel like a snitch."

*Robin, age seven*

"Mom wants me to live with her and Dad wants me to live with him. But I want to live with both of them. Why do I have to choose? I just want us to be happy again."

*Michael, age nine*

"Dad says Mom is divorcing us and doesn't love us any more because she has a boyfriend. Mom says Dad wasn't ever home and that she needed to feel loved by someone. I don't know who to believe any more. I don't think I trust anybody."

As you can see, children of divorce are the helpless victims of adult emotional entanglements. They need all the protection you can provide through this chaos to maintain a healthy self-esteem, trust in their parents, and a healthy attitude toward marriage and the family. Be careful with your decisions and interactions. Your children's future emotional well-being is at stake.

## CONSIDERING FINANCIAL AND PROPERTY ISSUES

In addition to decisions about custody and access, there are many more issues to be settled in the divorce procedure. Most of them deal with dividing up property, assets, and debts and deciding who will pay for what in the future.

These issues may be handled very differently from state to state. For example, in states with community property laws, all property and assets that are acquired during the marriage, as well as all debts, are typically divided and shared equally. Even money that you gained before the marriage may be subject to this community property interpretation if they were commingled with joint funds in the marriage. In other states these financial issues may be governed by other guidelines or negotiations. These issues can become very complicated, and you may need advice from an attorney or accountant to fully understand your requirements or choices.

We will try to identify some of the most prominent issues so you know what to expect. Some of these will be dealt with in more detail in the next chapter.

Spousal maintenance or alimony is a way to assist the spouse who has not worked or pursued a career during the marriage. The interpretation of this, as with all the following issues, will vary from state to state.

In the past, spousal maintenance was often awarded for long periods of time, perhaps until the children turned twenty-one or until that spouse remarried. Today the trend appears to be a specific temporary award to help the spouse complete schooling or gain additional training. For example, a wife who has been primarily a homemaker for the past ten years may say that she needs two years to complete her college work in teaching and one year to get established in a new job. Thus she would ask for three years of spousal maintenance. The actual monthly amount would be calculated according to her budget for personal and school expenses. Sometimes this support can also be offered in a lump-sum payment as part of the division of assets.

The decision to sell your house involves both financial and child-related issues. If possible, it's better to allow the children to remain in their house throughout the school year following the divorce. This provides them necessary stability and security.

Of course this is not always possible. Your choices here are pretty straightforward:

1. Sell the house and divide the equity (this is what a court will usually order if there is an unresolvable dispute).

2. One spouse buys out the other's half equity and becomes the sole owner. This is of course subject to mortgage requirements and the spouse's realistic ability to maintain the house.

3. Trade the equity in the house for other assets such as the value of a pension fund.

4. Both spouses can continue to co-own the house with one parent living in it until the children reach a certain age. At that time either the house would be sold or one parent would buy out the other. This is perhaps the least desirable because of the financial complication of co-owning the house.

Dividing financial assets involves adding up all your checking and savings accounts, investments (including such things as specially valued artworks or coin collections), and the value of your retirement plan accrued during the marriage. Sometimes all these funds will simply be divided on a fifty-fifty basis or they may be traded and balanced. For example, one spouse may want to keep certain stock investments and in trade will offer the other spouse a similar cash value from his or her savings. There are many ways to work these things out and negotiations can be as creative as the people involved.

We will discuss the division of personal property at some length in the next chapter. Basically, this involves dividing up personal belongings and household items that you and your spouse have acquired during the marriage. Often these decisions can become more emotional and painful than the financial ones. Sometimes valuable items and even furniture will need to be appraised if you and your spouse cannot agree on a fair division. Independent appraisers in your community can set a value on everything from your dining room set to your business.

The division of debts is handled similarly to dividing assets. All your bills, from local charge accounts to the mortgage on your house, must be added up and the amounts owed divided in a fair manner. Again this can be fifty-fifty or by a proportion based on your respective incomes, or one spouse can retain a certain debt to balance keeping other assets. For example, a wife who has made several valuable stock investments may want to keep them herself rather than sell or divide them with her husband. So she can offer to take over a proportion of the debt, such as paying off several credit card balances that would offset the value of the stocks.

The process is like creating a big ledger on which you and your spouse try to balance the assets and debts into a fair and reasonable settlement (see our model mediated agreement in Appendix C for more examples). But no matter what the legal requirements are in your state, the issue here is to be as fair and equitable with each other as possible. If one spouse feels cheated out of a fair share of assets, it can create animosity that lasts for years.

State and federal tax issues can become fairly complicated in divorces where the spouses are dividing a lot of assets and debts. For example, if in the divorce settlement your spouse transfers certain valuable properties to you, the transaction is typically not taxable and there are no losses or gains associated with it. But there *will* be future tax lia-bilities in selling this asset if it has gained in value in the meantime.

In general spousal maintenance is a tax deduction for the spouse who makes the payments and taxable income for the spouse receiving the payments. In contrast, child support is not federal taxable income for the parent receiving it nor a deduction for the parent paying it.

There are many variations of how this is interpreted for your state taxes. Only one parent can claim a child deduction on tax returns, and typically it's the parent who has physical custody. But there are many exceptions to this. The parent who contributes over half of the sup-port of the child may be eligible to claim the deduction, even though the child lives there less than half the time. Some parents who con-tribute fairly equally to the support of their children may decide to each claim a child. Again, there are many models, but these need to be addressed and negotiated at the time of the divorce.

Dealing with these financial and property issues in the divorce can seem overwhelming, and they can become even more difficult if you and your spouse and your attorneys get into a full-blown adversarial dispute. But it *is* possible, if your goal is to create a healthy divorce, to handle these matters in a straightforward manner. The outcome depends on the willingness of both spouses to work together. The next chapter will help you see the choices that you have.

# *6*

# Divorce: Collaboration or Gunfight

**N**O MATTER HOW successfully you and your spouse have worked through the first stages of preparation for divorce, you've now arrived at a critical turning point that will determine how the actual procedure will go forward.

Most divorcing couples in this country don't know that there are alternatives to the vindictive courtroom fight dramatized in movies and TV shows, where flamboyant and devious attorneys win through manipulation and dirty tricks.

You don't have to do it this way. There is an alternative: divorce mediation. This means that you and your spouse can sit down with a trained professional mediator and work out your own divorce agreement. This self-determined agreement can specify everything from the type of custody and access to matters of child support, spousal maintenance, and the fair division of property, assets, and debts. After all, you and your spouse know much more about the needs of your children than judges and attorneys, but it is they who will shape these decisions if you don't take an active role in this process.

So remember: The choice between a court battle and mediation can determine the relative potential for a healthy outcome to the actual divorce procedure. In this chapter, we tell you what to expect in both the adversarial and mediation alternatives. We also suggest professional resources for each. However, we want to be clear that we strongly favor mediation. Our years of experience with divorcing families have

## The Advantages of Mediating Your Divorce

1. You'll be able to express your concerns for the children as well as for your own needs following the divorce.

2. You'll be able to listen to your spouse's concerns in the same areas.

3. You'll be able to share ideas about what would work best for the children and how to handle certain financial issues.

4. The mediator will encourage, instruct, and manage, if necessary, your interactions so you can stay on track.

5. The mediator will diffuse intense or sensitive situations, unless by mutual consent you and your spouse need to share certain specific concerns.

6. The mediator will help you get "unstuck" in negotiations so you won't throw up your hands and walk away as you might at home.

7. The mediator will offer different ways to approach issues and new models that will make it easier to agree on issues or to accept tradeoffs.

convinced us that mediation is usually the most constructive and humane way to settle the many decisions related to divorce.

## STAGE 9
## MEDIATION—THE ART
## OF COLLABORATION

There will always be certain difficult and complex divorce disputes that will require the adversarial process and a judge to resolve, but we strongly believe that the great majority of divorces can be resolved effectively through mediation. The mediation experience will allow you and your spouse to sit in the same room, discuss your concerns,

8. The mediator will keep the interactions and negotiations balanced so that no one has an unfair advantage.

9. Some mediators may invite your children, depending on their ages and individual situation, to attend the final session to learn what you have worked out and to ask questions about what to expect. (We often invite adolescent children to cosign the mediated agreement. While it has no legal relevance, this helps the children feel more involved and support their parents' efforts to create this amicable settlement.)

10. Mediation is typically less costly than conducting the entire process through attorneys and certainly than going to a trial.

11. Mediation can usually accomplish a settlement much more quickly than adversarial procedures.

12. You will have an opportunity to have your agreement reviewed by an attorney before you sign it.

and create a mutually agreeable plan for issues of custody, access, and financial settlements.

Mediation is not like therapy, where you share underlying feelings and concerns in an effort to improve or repair your relationship. And it is not like arbitration, where both parties agree to abide by the arbitrator's rulings. Instead, mediation will provide you and your spouse a safe and structured setting where you can work together on mutual goals. The mediator will not let things get out of control as they might if you tried to do this alone. Mediation will provide you the healthiest alternative for finalizing your divorce. We have had some mediation clients tell us they communicated better during mediation than they had over the course of their entire marriage. Mediation also provides an educational experience with a professional who can discuss children's needs and issues as well as propose settlement models.

Many attorneys, judges, and therapists believe that mediation can work only in limited situations where both spouses are highly motivated and able to communicate without a lot of animosity. We disagree with this assumption. We have worked with cases as difficult as they come. Often attorneys call us with this kind of situation: "This couple has been divorced six years and they have been back to court five times. Would you be willing to try and mediate a settlement?" Once a judge called us to say, "I have a case I would like you to mediate but my recommendation is that you never see them at the same time in the same room. Good luck!"

The only prerequisite that we expect of mediation clients is that they are willing to sit down together for one session. Certainly some spouses who are more motivated for revenge will not be comfortable with this and prefer instead to pursue the adversarial direction. But we find that most parents, under their hurt and anger, share a genuine concern for protecting their children. This can be enough to provide the basis for successful mediation.

## WHO ARE MEDIATORS AND HOW DO YOU FIND THEM?

Most professional disciplines, such as medicine, psychotherapy, and law, have established formal programs of graduate education and specific requirements for supervised practice and experience. All these prerequisites must be met before professionals can be licensed or certified in your state. Unfortunately the field of mediation is so new that these kinds of requirements are still in a state of flux. No states in this country currently license mediators, and there are only a couple of masters' degree programs around the country that offer specific training in what they call "alternative dispute resolution." Most mediators learned their mediation skills from experience and working with colleagues. More recently, professionals wanting training in mediation may learn through apprenticeships or by being supervised by other senior mediators.

The primary professional organization for mediators who work with divorcing families is called the Academy of Family Mediators (see Appendix B). However, many experienced mediators do not belong to this organization, so when you look for a mediator you need to ask about experience.

Mediators basically come from two very different backgrounds—therapy and law. For many therapists, it's a relatively easy transition to use their counseling skills in the mediation process. On the other hand, many attorneys who become dissatisfied with the adversarial process move into doing mediation by using their knowledge of business and tax issues and their negotiation skills.

There are many competent mediators from both fields, but there are a few differences you may want to consider. If in your divorce you are very concerned about your children and need professional suggestions about what would work best for them, then you should seek a mediator with a therapy background. If you are primarily concerned about complicated business and financial issues, then you may want to consider a mediator with a legal background.

## HOW DOES MEDIATION WORK?

All mediators have their own style and focus. It might be helpful to look first at our model mediated divorce agreement in Appendix C at the end of the book. This will give you an idea of what you can accomplish at the conclusion of mediation. However, to help you gain a sense of what to expect, here we briefly walk through a model experience.

We normally insist that both spouses come in together for the first session. This communicates a message that they are both willing to interact and work together, and that we can manage their potential conflict. It also lets them know how important it is for them to participate in this experience together. Normally the entire mediation will be conducted in these joint sessions. If there are either confusing issues or hotly debated concerns, however, we may meet with each spouse once or twice individually simply to clarify their positions and to help diffuse the intensity of their stance.

It has been our experience over the years that it's more effective—both logistically and emotionally—to mediate issues about the children first. Resolving these issues often allows the resolution of financial concerns to occur much more smoothly.

We begin by asking both parents to tell us a little about their family and the roles that each played in parenting. Then we have them tell us about each of their children. After this, we ask both parents to let us know in their own words what they think would work best for their children in terms of living in each household. At this point, we often comment on what we think works best with children of this age.

After they've talked about access issues we often spend time doing some education about models of custody, much as you have read at the beginning of Chapter Five. If there are concerns about control issues, the ability to make parental decisions, or either spouse's parenting skills, we will take time to discuss these. Here we try to separate the leftover marital issues, hurts, and anger from the realistic issues that will affect parenting the children. If interactions become tense, we help the parents back up and learn how to say what they intend without becoming hostile.

Often the first few one-hour sessions are spent educating parents about their choices and what these mean to their children, and helping them learn to separate their emotional and marital issues from choices about custody or access. In a few rare cases where the animosity between the parents is volatile, we may suspend the mediation and either set aside a few individual sessions with one of us or refer them to a colleague to help clear out unhealthy emotional baggage. We often tell parents they need to get these emotional issues settled and out of the way or they'll still be carrying this into their relationships with their children five or ten years from now.

After the second session we begin to outline a preliminary agreement; we use a word processor so they can take a draft home and review it after each session. Within a few sessions the access plan, summer and holiday plans, and definition of custody are usually formalized. If there are areas they need time to think about, then we simply come back to them rather than push for an agreement prematurely. Remember, the goal is for both parents to feel that this agreement is both fair and equitable.

We then take care of the financial areas related to the children, namely child support, dental and health care insurance, beneficiaries on life insurance, and tax issues. From here we ask parents to prepare a detailed list of their assets and debts. Once parents see these outlined in front of them, it's easier to decide how to divide them up. Usually the biggest issue with most couples is their house. The house represents not only their biggest asset and liability but also their strongest issues of emotional attachment. Often there can be tradeoffs. For example, one parent may keep the house and its equity in trade for the other parent's retaining the value of their retirement plan or other investments. If you feel that you are not as good at negotiating financial areas as your spouse, don't worry: it's the mediator's responsibility to make sure the negotiations are equitable and balanced.

We usually save the division of personal property until last because these items often carry a lot of emotional investment. It's easier to divide them up after the child-related decisions and other financial matters have been resolved. We suggest that parents dividing up personal property walk through their household together at a time when the children are not at home. We suggest they list items in three columns—items you want to have at all costs, items you would like but are willing to negotiate about, and items you don't want. If both people make their own list at the same time, probably 60 to 75 percent of all the items will be settled.

We have included an example of what a list might look like.

## Dividing Up Personal Property

| HAVE TO HAVE AT ALL COSTS | NEGOTIABLE | DO NOT WANT |
| --- | --- | --- |
| stereo | television | tools |
| bedroom set | dining set | second television |
| living room pictures | couch/chairs | furniture in den |
| silverware | hallway pictures | old dinner plates |
| washer/dryer | blender | ice maker |
| microwave | refrigerator | |

If couples have valuable collections, of art or stamps, for example, these items may need to be appraised independently. But we find most couples can avoid this added expense. Also remember that most household items are appraised at their resale value, not at the original purchase price or replacement cost.

As the agreement falls into place, we print out a copy and recommend that both spouses sit down with an attorney to review it before signing. We recommend family-law attorneys who we know are willing to work with mediated agreements on an hourly fee. This avoids a large retainer since there will probably not be a dispute. An attorney will go over technical issues and advise the spouses about their legal rights, and will call the mediator if questions arise. Occasionally, where we have questions about technical legal issues or tax matters we identify them for both spouses to discuss with their attorneys.

When this step is complete, the couple sign and return what we call a memorandum of understanding, and we cosign it. This is not yet a legal contract until one of the attorneys files it with the dissolution papers, but it does represent the mediated agreement.

Occasionally there are certain items that a couple just cannot agree on. This need not invalidate the mediation process. The mediated agreement is written with all of the items that *have* been agreed to, and the couple will have to rely on their attorneys to either negotiate or litigate the remaining issues. Often with a mediated divorce agreement even three-fourths complete, attorneys are able to work out the remainder of the items. Sometimes a couple can decide on everything about the children but just can't settle the division of property. If they have to go to court over these financial issues the agreements about the children will usually remain intact.

Overall, there are very few drawbacks in the mediation experience. It is what we often refer to as a win-win situation. The children win because their parents are working toward a plan that is in their best interest and their fate is not being decided by a judge who has never met them. The parents win because they are dealing with each other, learning some new communication skills that will follow them into their postdivorce co-parenting experiences, and saving themselves the humiliating experience of attacking and demeaning one another in a courtroom battle (not to mention those staggering legal bills). The attorneys win because they can work with cooperative clients who can benefit from their legal resources. The judges and courts win because they are not forced to make Solomon-like decisions about children and because every successfully mediated case represents a reduction of their overburdened case calendar.

---

# STAGE 10
# THE ADVERSARIAL
# DIVORCE—GUNFIGHT
# AT THE OK CORRAL

While we want you to consider healthier alternatives to an adversarial divorce, we also realize that not all differences can be negotiated or mediated. We find very few issues about custody and access that can't be worked out when both parents step back and commit to being reasonable for the children's sake. However, when one or both parents are unwilling to be reasonable, then a judge may need to make a final decision.

Similarly, complicated financial and property disputes cannot always be fairly negotiated, and when attorneys cannot sort them out a judge may have to make a final ruling. So when all other possible solutions have been exhausted, there *is* a place for the court in divorce matters. We want you to anticipate what to expect and be prepared to make some healthy choices.

## SELECTING AN ATTORNEY

The first step in selecting an attorney is to identify someone who is competent in family law and whom you can trust and work with comfortably. We cannot emphasize too strongly that you need to select an attorney who specializes in family law. The legal field has become just as specialized as the medical field. Some attorneys may spend their entire careers in tax or real estate law, for example, and never even enter a courtroom.

We have seen many unfair judgments in courtrooms because the attorneys were inexperienced in family law. While they are no doubt excellent in their special field, they won't always know how to present the issues in a custody dispute. So remember: If you are suffering from hemorrhoids you wouldn't go to a neurosurgeon for treatment. If you're getting divorced, don't go to a personal-injury lawyer or a maritime attorney.

Probably the best way to locate family-law attorneys is to ask for referrals from your therapist or mediator, from a minister or rabbi, or from friends who've been satisfied with a certain attorney in their own divorce. The next choice is to check in the Yellow Pages under Divorce or Matrimonial Attorneys or call the local bar association for a list of attorneys who specialize in divorce issues.

In selecting an attorney, remember that she or he will be your employee. You are paying this person's fees, so as the consumer you have the right to ask questions and decide if you can work comfortably together. Here are some questions that will help you select an attorney who'll be appropriate for your needs.

1. How long have you been in practice?

2. What percent of your practice is related to divorce issues?

3. How many times have you been to trial in divorce cases?

4. Do you work with divorce mediators? How do you feel about divorce mediators?

5. How do you feel about joint custody?

6. Have you worked with divorces involving young children?

7. Have you worked with clients who have the kind of business that we have?

8. Have you worked with divorces that involved retirement benefits (or other types of unusual concerns pertinent to your individual situation)?

There is another area to consider: personal style. Do you want an attorney who is aggressive and confrontive or one who is more conciliatory? Not everyone needs the aggressive attorney who makes threats and tries to intimidate the other side. Many soft-spoken, thoughtful attorneys can represent you competently and effectively, and not alienate everyone around you. If you feel that your spouse will try to intimidate or take unfair advantage of you, however, you may want a more aggressive attorney. Most of all, you need to select someone you can trust and are personally comfortable with.

## HOW THE ADVERSARIAL PROCESS WORKS

If you are the spouse who is leaving the relationship, then you'll probably be the first one to consult an attorney and the one to file the papers. This simply means that your attorney will file the initial petition for divorce or marital dissolution. According to the requirements of the state in which you live, this document will define the grounds or reasons for the divorce.

Most states now have what is called no-fault divorce. In the past one spouse had to prove in court— often by using private investigators or other secretive means—that the other spouse was an adulterer, a drug addict, or an abusive person. For the judge to grant a divorce, it was necessary that "fault" be found.

The no-fault divorce, on the other hand, recognizes that many relationships simply end without someone having to be at fault or the bad guy. It represents an effort to reduce the adversarial nature of the divorce procedure and it has been a major change for the better in the way courts view divorcing spouses. The grounds for no-fault divorces, for example, are usually stated as "irretrievable breakdown of the marriage" (Arizona, Georgia, Hawaii, Florida, Indiana), "irreconcilable differences" (California, Illinois, Idaho, Mississippi), or "incompatibility" (Kansas, Nevada). Today most states have certain provisions for a no-fault divorce.

Most states require a waiting period, which begins after your attorney files the petition and it has been served on your spouse. In Arizona, for example, it's sixty days. This means that the divorce cannot be finalized until the end of that period. During this time you, your spouse, and your attorneys will maneuver back and forth in an effort to reach a satisfactory settlement in the hope that you won't have to go to court for a trial.

In the petition that your attorney filed there is usually a preliminary statement of what you want, such as the type of custody, financial support, spousal maintenance, and so on. This is the beginning of the bargaining process. For instance, you may tell your attorney that you would be happy with joint custody, but he may say, "Let's put down sole custody so we can use it to bargain for spousal maintenance" or you may say, "I want my children to live with their mother during the school week because I travel so much and I would like to have them on weekends." And your attorney may suggest, "Let's ask for them to live with you and we can negotiate this so she doesn't try to get half of your business assets."

Attorneys spend many years in law school learning how to protect the best interests of their clients. This means learning how to be adversarial—treating the people on the "other side" as enemies. An adversarial attorney may also advise you to throw your spouse out of the house, send your children out of town, change the locks on your house, or take all the money out of joint accounts.

This illustrates how the role of attorneys begins to escalate the adversarial process. Your attorney is maneuvering to protect your situation, so that you will have more to bargain with later. In the process, issues about the needs of your children become secondary. If you and your husband had previously discussed joint custody, you can imagine the shock and anger when he receives the papers stating that you want sole custody. He may feel betrayed and angry, hire a nasty attorney, and begin the process of revenge.

This is just a mild example of how quickly the legal process can turn you and your spouse into enemies. Your attorneys are doing what they are trained to do, but you need to remind them that they work for you and you don't want to escalate the divorce into a vindictive battleground.

Most experienced family-law attorneys will do their best to negotiate a settlement with your spouse's attorney so that you will not have to go to a trial. You will be asked to prioritize the issues, deciding what aspects of the custody, access, and financial questions are the most important. You may be asked by either your attorney or your spouse's to fill out lengthy forms and provide extensive information about things from everyday budgets to several years of income tax returns. This is a legal process called "discovery," where attorneys determine the actual assets that both of you have and the relative costs of your lifestyles. These financial facts will be used in attempts to reach a settlement or when you are questioned in a trial.

Even though there is a minimum waiting period, this does not mean that the divorce will be finalized at the end of that time—unless the divorce is "uncontested" or all the disputes are worked out in detail. Many divorces take much longer. If you must go to trial you may have to wait six months in some states just to get a trial date. Many states, such as New York, have much longer waiting periods. There is also the possibility that the trial will be "continued" (meaning delayed) to an even later date.

There's always the possibility of a settlement during lengthy delays. However, be aware that some attorneys may drag the process out deliberately, hoping that the financial needs of the other spouse will turn the climate toward concessions. Also, in some cases the longer it takes, the larger the attorney's fees. Be aware of the fact that because it is very time consuming to prepare for trial, attorneys make a great deal of money when they go into court. So some unscrupulous attorneys will be hell bent to go to trial.

Many other things can delay the process. You may need to determine exactly what your joint assets are. You may have to have your home or other valuable property appraised if it's to be sold or if its value will be used in the negotiations. You may have to wait for detailed statements about the value in retirement plans. You can imagine the expensive time it takes for your attorney to talk to you about an issue, send a proposal for resolving that issue to the other attorney, for that attorney to review the proposal with your spouse, then communicate an alternative proposal with your attorney, who then schedules a meeting with you to go over it. Obviously, the more you and your spouse are able to communicate with each other through this process, the quicker it will be resolved.

## THE ROLE OF THE JUDGE

Unfortunately, when couples decide to end their marriage, they are thrown into the same legal arena that was designed for proving the innocence or guilt of people charged with criminal offenses. Most judges do not relish making decisions and writing orders about custody disputes. They literally feel like the biblical Solomon, who finally suggested slicing the disputed child in half to determine who the real mother was. When we worked with the Conciliation Court in our city a number of years ago, we sat in many judges' chambers consulting with them while they agonized over what choices were in the best interest of the children in divorce cases before them.

Unlike criminal cases, where a judge can weigh the evidence and make an informed decision about guilt or innocence, in most divorce cases both parents may be healthy, functioning, competent individuals and parents. So there are often no easy solutions to deciding which is the better parent. And not all judges are necessarily wise and sensitive to emotional and developmental issues. Many would rather be trying more glamorous criminal cases with clear issues of guilt or innocence. Others may not have the patience to sort through what they may perceive as petty complaints between spouses. And still others may be guided more by their own personal biases in these family matters than by the legal issues or by notions of what is fair and just.

For example, several years ago it was a joke around the courthouse that one of the judges who had been taken to the cleaners by his wife in his own divorce six months earlier had not ruled in favor of the mother gaining custody in a single case since then. Another quite elderly judge, who was very biased in favor of only mothers having custody of young children, fell asleep while Craig was on the witness stand testifying about his concerns regarding the mother's history of alcoholism and neglect. The mother was awarded sole custody primarily because of this judge's biases and because the father was represented by a tax attorney friend who had never been to trial in a divorce case.

We have other horror stories that we sometimes tell clients who believe they'll walk into court and get everything they ask for, including the private satisfaction that the other parent has been publicly humiliated. Many attorneys will promise clients everything they want, knowing full well that on any given day with any given judge the outcome will be a gamble.

In many courtroom battles your odds of emerging the victor may be no better than fifty-fifty. *There are no guarantees when you go to court.* And while there may be a winner on paper, everyone is a loser emotionally. We often tell our clients who want to do battle: "There is no way you and your spouse can go into court and demean each other in a battle over the children and walk away with any future respect for each other as parents or any ability to cooperate in raising the children."

Gradually, however, the courts have become somewhat more sensitive to the emotional needs of children and more educated about the valuable role of *both* parents in children's adjustment after the divorce. Now judges and attorneys rely more on therapists to evaluate parents and children and make recommendations in custody disputes.

## UNDERSTANDING A CUSTODY EVALUATION

If you are proceeding through this adversarial route and cannot reach an agreement about your children, a custody evaluation is often considered. This can be a healthy option, because it brings into the picture an experienced professional who will be aware of the emotional needs and dilemmas of children whose parents are divorcing. This professional should be experienced in one of the mental health fields and preferably trained in working with families and children.

If your divorce is headed toward a trial, the alternative to this custody evaluation is the traditional adversarial approach where both parents bring in what are known as "expert witnesses" to testify on their behalf. In this route, your attorney will have you meet with a therapist to evaluate your personal history and parenting resources and skills. This therapist probably will not meet with your spouse and may not spend more than an hour with your children. Your spouse will meet similarly with another therapist. In most cases both therapists will testify that the person they evaluated can function well as a parent. If one of the therapists cannot support the client then the attorney will find another one who can. You may have heard of people who testify this way being called hired guns. The usual effect is that they cancel each other out and the judge still has to make a subjective decision.

We began advising attorneys nearly fifteen years ago that we would evaluate parents in custody cases only if we could have access to everyone in the family— both parents, all the children, including stepchildren if present, grandparents if necessary, and even live-in partners and roommates. We didn't feel it was either realistic or ethical for professionals to speculate and make judgments about which parents would be best for custody without having evaluated everyone involved in the family system. We began conducting independent family custody evaluations, where we did not represent one parent or the other but, acting as what the legal system refers to as a "friend of the court," offered impartial recommendations.

In your community these custody evaluations may be offered by a court-related program such as a conciliation court as well as by private therapists. You need a professional to be truly independent, someone who has not known or worked with anyone in your family and has no special ties to either of the attorneys. In most cases the cost will be divided equally or proportionately between the parents. Sometimes one parent agrees to pay for the entire evaluation because he or she feels it is more important than the other parent does.

The actual evaluation conducted will vary with each evaluator. We do these evaluations as a team because it adds a female and male perspective to our observations. It also helps us be more objective and thorough, and it blends Sandy's expertise with children and Craig's expertise with marriages and families into an effective evaluation. We have described our model in professional journals and know of other programs around the country that offer team evaluations. However, in most cases each of you will be interviewed by one therapist.

Some evaluators will have you take certain psychological tests, such as the Minnesota Multiphasic Personality Inventory (MMPI). These tests are designed to identify underlying psychopathology. We don't use them regularly unless we are concerned about a parent displaying severe symptoms that may be of a psychiatric nature. On the contrary, we believe that most parents disputing custody are basically normal individuals who may occasionally display dysfunctional symptoms because of the extreme stress and pressures of divorcing.

In any case, so you'll know what to expect in a custody evaluation, we'll describe how we do it. First Craig spends two sessions, totaling about two hours, with each parent individually, evaluating everything from the models of parenting and family interaction the parents learned from their own families of origin to their dating patterns, marital interactions, parenting roles, involvement and attachment to the children, and abilities to understand the developmental needs of each child. Next Sandy will interview the children, either together or separately depending on their ages, to determine where they are emotionally and developmentally, to understand how they view and are handling the divorce, and to evaluate the quality of their relationship with each of their parents.

It's important to note that children are *never* asked in any of these interviews whom they want to live with. They are asked about what it's like to be with each of their parents, how they are alike and how they are different. They are asked about being with each of their parents on weekdays and weekends and what they like to do with each of them. Sometimes, children do volunteer that they want to live with one or the other. If so, then they're asked why they have these preferences and whether anyone told them to say this.

Then Sandy will see the children in a play situation with each parent separately. This gives her a chance to observe how the parent relates to and manages the children as well as how the children respond to each parent. Often we will meet with the parents together to give them some feedback about concerns we might have or to make suggestions about helping the children deal with the divorce.

Finally, we will advise them of our findings and what we plan to recommend. Sometimes our recommendations provide the basis for a formal agreement between the two parents, and they don't have to go to trial. Other times one parent may be unhappy with our recommendations and challenge our findings. In that case we appear in court and answer questions from both attorneys explaining and defending our recommendations. Then the judge may use our recommendations as well as his or her own observations to make a ruling.

The significance of the custody evaluation is that it provides to the adversarial system—a system that is not equipped to recognize these issues—professional and impartial input about the children's needs and the parents' resources. It is important to remember that there are no courses in law schools about child development, family dynamics, or abnormal psychology.

The choice of a mediated or adversarial divorce is yours. We have identified the pros and cons of each. We have also stated our belief that all divorcing spouses should attempt mediation before going to court. Not every divorce can be mediated, but most can. We hope this discussion gives you some direction and some confidence that you can be in control of your own destiny.

# 7

# Co-Parenting After Divorce: A Cold War or a New Beginning

THE DIVORCE IS OVER!

There are no more attorneys in your life. The decisions have been made. You can't go back. Whether you worked out a mutual agreement with your former spouse or had a judge impose a final settlement, it's done and filed as a legal contract.

Now you have to make it work for your children and for yourself. Now you have to let go of all the hostile baggage that the divorce created.

Whatever your fantasies or fears were earlier in the divorce process, they'll come into focus now with the reality of being on your own. The next stages will be critical in defining patterns of interaction that can last a lifetime for you, your former spouse, and your children. To complete the divorce experience in a healthy manner, this postdivorce time should be a new beginning for everyone in the family. Unfortunately, for many families after divorce, the experience often feels like a cold war with occasional hot skirmishes.

Our intention is to help you avoid a cold war and create a new beginning for yourself, full of optimism and possibilities. So in this and the next two chapters let's consider the concluding stages, which deal with postdivorce co-parenting, remarriage, and blended families (stepfamilies).

## STAGE 11
## CO-PARENTING AFTER
## THE DIVORCE

Completing this stage in a healthy manner depends on two important factors. The first is redefining and restructuring the parental roles and duties that now exist in two households. Second is your personal adjustment, how successfully you'll be able to let go of your former marriage and go on with your life.

We have found that the children's emotional adjustment during the postdivorce period will be linked directly to your own personal adjustment. This is extremely important to remember.

In our experience the healthy resolution of this postdivorce stage of co-parenting involves working on tasks in three areas simultaneously:

1. Managing separate households

2. Reconnecting as single co-parents with your former spouse

3. Developing new social ties for yourself as a single adult

### MANAGING SEPARATE HOUSEHOLDS

From the time of your original separation, you, your former spouse, and the children began the uncertain struggle of defining a new, two-household family structure. Before the separation there was only one household, and you knew where everything and everybody was supposed to be. Everyone's primary identity and the life of the family revolved around that household.

But this issue of recognizing and managing the logistics associated with two households creates confusion and difficulties for divorced families. Unfortunately, not having clear roles or expectations often leads parents into unpleasant and angry power struggles over the children's time and loyalties.

It is crucial for parents to step back and recognize that each new household is going to be different. The old household can never exist again, no matter how hard you try to duplicate it. If one parent has the fantasy that everything should remain the same for the sake of the children, then any changes in lifestyle that the other parent introduces will meet with an immediate challenge.

Craig recently met with a couple that had been divorced less than a year and neither parent had become seriously involved with new partners yet. The father complained that the mother was too strict with "his" eleven-year-old son and too lenient with their eight-year-old daughter. He felt the son had unrealistic chores and responsibilities in the mother's household. He also objected to the mother's recently acquired antique furniture. He said that the children complained that it was uncomfortable to sit on and they always had to be careful about breaking something fragile. The mother was less intrusive about the father's household except to say that the children had reported that it was dirty and they always had to help him clean it. Neither parent had been in the other's household since the divorce.

Each of your new environments should be comfortable and attractive extensions of yourselves. This will probably mean something different from what it used to be like. Perhaps your style and tastes are changing, perhaps you never really expressed your preferences while you were married. Try to be supportive of each other and not see the changes as a threat.

We have already talked about the fact that the divorce decree should spell out the specifics of access—when the children will be in your home and when they'll be at the other parent's home. For the first year after the divorce it's particularly important for your children to maintain a regular schedule at the two homes. You may want to agree to certain adjustments, but do them gradually and let the children know about any changes several weeks in advance. Remember, to feel secure, children need consistency.

Try to respect the other parent's time and schedule. Make it a policy to pick up and return children *on time*. If you are going to be late, call and let the other parent know. If you are going to be out of town or unable to take the children for your scheduled time, let the other parent know as far in advance as possible and make up with future times whenever you can.

Make it a policy not to comment on the other parent's household or lifestyle—the color of the carpet, the size of the TV, the style of the furniture. If the children want to complain, tell them to talk to the other parent about these issues, not you. Don't get pulled into judging or criticizing the other parent's decisions or parenting choices. You have enough to work on with your own parenting. The children don't need to be caught in the middle of power struggles.

## HELPING YOUR CHILDREN

The children's going back and forth between two households is perhaps the most difficult issue parents struggle with in the early postdivorce period. It seems to be especially difficult for mothers, since they often have become accustomed to having exclusive control of their children's environment and primary parenting responsibility. Suddenly they're in a situation where for long periods of time they are out of contact with the children. They cannot dictate what will happen to them, where they go, or who they're with. It is frightening for many mothers, especially those who tend to be overprotective or who have developed overly close bonds with their children. As they attempt to control these parenting choices in their former spouse's home, they're often met with resentment. They may be told they're being intrusive and overcontrolling. Often the more they struggle with this dilemma the more the other parent resists sharing any information about the children's time away from them.

Unfortunately, this is one of those "everybody's right and everybody's wrong" situations. The mother is trying to continue to protect the children and make sure they are parented "correctly" (that is, the way she does it). The father is trying to establish a quality, independent relationship and develop his own style of parenting, sometimes with a paucity of parenting experience behind him. This minimal experience may lead him to be oversensitive about advice or criticism in the parenting area. And the mother may see this as being defensive and secretive.

Another common complicating factor is that often fathers become far better parents (more attentive and caring) after a divorce than they were before. Mothers often see fathers as having been terrible parents before the divorce, who never disciplined, were never home, and were never there for the kids. Suddenly these fathers are asking for equal time, wanting to attend everything the child does and challenging the mother's parenting choices when "before" they were perfectly happy with them. The resentment and anger created by this common scenario are very difficult for mothers to get beyond. And often the early attempts at control are, in actuality, manifestations of their resentment and anger.

To complicate matters even further, postdivorce parenting becomes especially tense if a new adult companion enters the picture early or if there was one in the background when the divorce occurred. The most painful, threatening aspect for parents in this stage is the enormous fear of another person mothering or fathering their children. The panic of believing you might be replaced as a mother or father is extremely common, and is very strong stuff indeed!

But please believe us when we tell you: If you are a good parent—loving, attentive, and consistent in your time with the children—no one can replace you or substitute for you in your children's eyes. *Parents are not replaceable parts!*

Children are totally amazed by this fear that their parents experience. They listen to us explain this worry and cannot grasp how parents could ever think children could replace them no matter how much they like or even love a stepparent. Michael, age ten, said, "You're kidding! My dad thinks I'll stop loving him just because my mom is going to marry Jim? He's my *dad*. What a dumb idea!"

The only possible exception is a situation where a child was younger than four when you separated and your time with the child after the divorce was sparse or unpredictable. Under these circumstances, sometimes a stronger bond can exist with a stepparent who came on the scene early in the child's life and who was a very good parenting figure.

Beyond this issue of worrying about being replaced is the more difficult issue of another person's values, beliefs, and personality style being imposed on your children. If the new adult was part of a marital affair, the feelings of resentment and the level of reactivity to their involvement with the children are, of course, even greater.

All these issues are really about sharing power and control of the children. It's a difficult adjustment to let go of all the anxiety and need to control for the sake of the children's future healthy adjustments. But you must.

How do you go about doing this? First, you must truly believe that it's in your children's best interest to have a quality relationship with *both* parents. This attitude about sharing your children will be communicated very clearly to them and will affect their attitude about changing homes. If you believe that the children need only *one* home and the other home is where they go to "visit" the other parent, this belief will slowly undermine the children's comfort with living in two homes.

### Reminders to Help You Help Your Children After the Divorce

1. Do not demean the other parent's living situation, eating habits, choice of friends, choice of activities, choice of dates, or parenting decisions. If you have concerns, speak to the other parent personally, far away from the children's hearing.

2. Help the children explore their own feelings without influencing them with your own. If positive comments seem impossible, neutral statements about the other parent are better than negative ones.

3. Do not encourage, in any manner, the children to be spies or tattlers on the other parent. This can cause a lot of guilty feelings and loyalty conflicts.

4. Assist in dividing the children's things so they will be comfortable in both homes.

5. Don't let the children manipulate or play you off against each other. All children will try this at some point. If there is continuing hostility between parents, the chances for this manipulation to work are greatly improved.

Attitude is 90 percent of the ability to adapt for both parents and children. Children are amazingly adaptable, usually far more than their parents. They can, over time, become used to differences in parenting styles and values, differing lifestyles, and a range of discipline methods. This adaptation process will take some time. During the initial phase, you are likely to see some frustration and certainly some testing of limits in the children's behavior. It's important that you view these changes as temporary, as part of the children's adjustment to the divorce.

How long it will take varies with the individual child and with each family's unique history. The normal range would be from about two months to about two years. The faster the parents develop a pre-

6. Be honest with your children but don't burden them with more than they can handle, emotionally or developmentally.

7. Work hard to develop a positive, enthusiastic, optimistic attitude about your custody and access structure. Your attitude will greatly influence your children's attitude.

8. Do not disappoint your children by being inconsistent or unpredictable. Stable routine is important. Children are very hurt if you cancel time with them, show up late to pick them up, or bring them back earlier than planned.

9. Learn to share your children comfortably. Give up the need to be intrusive into your former spouse's life or to control what she does with the children. Try to develop trust in her as a parent, even if you have lost trust in her as spouse or friend.

10. Learn to rebuild your life into one where you are growing in new directions, where you have become happy with yourself, and where you are optimistic about the future. Your sense of well-being and hope will affect your children's adjustment in wonderful ways.

dictable, stable sharing plan and the better they're able to give up their power struggles and animosity, the faster and easier will be the children's process of adjustment and adaptation.

Our strong belief, supported by many years of research, is that children need a quality, ongoing relationship with *both* their parents after a divorce. Whatever your spouse's limitations or deficits—short of actually abusing or endangering a child—children need both their parents on a meaningful basis after a divorce. You must accept the idea that even though you may not agree with your ex-spouse in many areas of life or parenting choices, he is still the only other parent your children will ever have. Children may endure significant emotional damage if a relationship with that parent is denied or severely limited.

Listen to Lisa, an angry, confused sixteen-year-old in therapy for depression, who screamed out her pain during our session:

I'll never forgive my mother for keeping me from my father. She did everything she could to turn us against him. She said he didn't love us and never called but never told us she'd changed our number to unlisted and never given us the letters he wrote or the packages he sent. He finally gave up trying after we moved three times. How could she do that to me? I spent eight years without a father, thinking he didn't love me, all because she hated him for leaving with another woman.

Or Adam, a twelve-year-old runaway, who was seen at the request of a social worker at a group home:

After the divorce, I only got to see my mom every other weekend because she was living with her boyfriend. After a while, I felt like a stranger. We hardly knew each other any more. She didn't really understand what was going on in my life and I didn't know much about hers. We could hardly talk. We finally just gave up trying and saw each other less and less. My dad wouldn't let me go over there more often because he was always mad at her and running her down. I ran away because it didn't seem to me like either one of them really cared about me. All they cared about was getting even with each other.

## RECONNECTING AS SINGLE CO-PARENTS

One of the most difficult aspects of co-parenting is learning to be parents when you are no longer lovers and partners. Both of you will be challenged to redefine your roles with each other as parents. This is one of the most important areas for you to master if your children are going to be able to get through the divorce in a healthy manner.

No matter what form of custody you have, no matter what division of the children's time has been developed, you and your former spouse need to define a shared and respectful role as parents. Neither of you can cease to be a quality parent!

Remember, children have a terrible fear that they'll lose one or both parents. To the extent that you and your former spouse continue to

battle or end up in a cold-war power struggle, the children are emotionally losing both of you. They need their life to be as settled,
secure, and predictable as possible after the divorce.

This means, as we've said before, that children should never be used
as go-betweens to carry messages between the parents. Part of defining
your postdivorce relationship will involve learning how to communicate with each other while leaving the former marital issues behind. If
you were fortunate enough to have mediated your divorce, then you
likely have learned some new communication skills and will be more
comfortable interacting with your former spouse. If you went through
an adversarial divorce experience, then the task of repairing the
unpleasantness and regaining trust for each other may take some time
and be more of a struggle.

We suggest that about six months after the divorce has been finalized, you and your former spouse sit down quietly for lunch and begin
to discuss the children and your parenting roles. If this suggestion
sounds overwhelming or impossible, if so much anger or hurt is still
left, then you need some help. Find a family therapist who specializes
in divorce and will know how to help you. Perhaps a support group
such as Divorce Recovery or Parents Without Partners can also be
helpful. You and your former spouse need to start talking reasonably
about the children within six months—not two years.

## FRIENDS AND RELATIVES AFTER THE DIVORCE

Divorce causes reverberations and repercussions throughout the entire
spectrum of your social network. When it occurs with a couple who
had put up a good front around friends, family, and even children, the
effects are even stronger and longer lasting for those around them.

Divorce shakes the foundations of many people's value and belief
systems. It threatens the very core of their own stability. So it will be
difficult for people around you to stay neutral and objective about the
events surrounding a divorce. Loyalty issues become more pro-
nounced as people take sides and decide who was right or wrong,
good or bad. Friends who have rough spots in their own marriage may
be threatened by your divorce or encouraged by it to tread dangerous
waters in their own relationships.

Part of what you must accept is that because of the anxiety, threat,
confusion, anger, fear, and dread that those around you may feel, you

will lose many social acquaintances and even some of your close friends, including some family members. They will drift away, uncomfortable with the new "uncoupled" you and confused about how to interact with you in your new role of single and divorced. Or they may choose instead to side with your former spouse because of loyalties or similarity of interests.

This experience of losing long-term friends even family members is one of the most difficult realities of getting divorced. It is a shock to many people that these friendships are so easily lost, and it is a very painful part of the grieving process.

When the divorce has been extremely hostile or one or both spouses are really hurting, friends may also feel the need to be supportive by aligning with the one they were closest to and being critical of the other. So when your friend sides with you and her husband sides with your former husband you can imagine the conflict they may experience. Often, their inability to resolve these loyalty issues and remain neutral causes them to drift away from you because it creates too many problems in their own relationship. Even with more distant friends your divorce can be very threatening to many couples. "If it could happen to them, it could happen to us" is a frightening reality. People prefer not to deal with that reality because it is too scary and often distance themselves so they're not reminded of how easily a marriage can deteriorate.

Occasionally your friends may become angry with you for getting a divorce because it creates a significant loss for them. They can no longer enjoy a friendship with you and your spouse. Social occasions change dramatically with only one of you present. It can also be uncomfortable for them when either of you begins to date and they must learn to restructure your long-standing friendship to include a new adult with no shared history. They may not like or approve of this new companion.

Unfortunately, it is fairly rare for a couple or married friend to stay neutral or maintain quality, ongoing relationships with both you and your former spouse. Some friends attempt it at first but generally— and usually in a short period of time—will either give up their friendship with both or will choose to remain close to one spouse while distancing from the other.

In-law relationships can be even more fragile. When a couple choose to end their marriage they often feel the need to walk away from all the family members that came to them through marriage. These can be very painful losses for adults and for children. It is especially cruel to children who have known these people as members of their family all their lives and who feel abandoned by them.

We are close friends with a couple who divorced after fifteen years of marriage. The husband announced quite suddenly that he was bored, tired of the marriage, and moving out. He was also involved with another woman. Despite the fact that for fifteen years he had close relationships with his brother-in-law and his wife and their children, after moving out he never spoke to any of them again or they to him. Four years later, these teenage children are still angry and confused that their uncle simply wrote them off.

It is possible to attempt to preserve some of these important relationships, but despite the best efforts it may not be possible to salvage them all. It's often helpful to give friends permission to be close to both of you. Tell them openly that they don't need to take sides. You can make efforts to stay in touch with them, even those who had a stronger friendship with your former spouse.

Even if the spouse's family had been openly hostile, but especially if they were not, make an early effort to tell them that you have not divorced them and that maintaining your and your children's relationships with them is very important to you. Don't encourage them to be openly critical of their own family member, since the underlying resentment of this stance may cause them eventually to distance from you. Similarly, with friends, don't encourage alignments against your former spouse or put them in the awkward position of playing judge and jury. They might find this very uncomfortable and avoid contact with you so they do not have to deal with these conflicts of loyalty.

In your new role as a single person you have to reach out to these former friends and in-laws far more than you may have needed to in the past since they'll be contending with a host of conflicting, confusing, awkward feelings. Invite them over for small get-togethers, call them for pleasant (that is, *not* divorce-related) conversations, make plans to get together with one or both of them to engage in familiar activities. In every way you can, let them know you don't want to lose them from your life.

If you have children, it is especially important that you try to hold on to the relationships formed with your former spouse's family. These people are their grandparents, uncles, aunts, and cousins. Losing these important relationships would constitute a great hardship for them. Even if your effort is met with a somewhat guarded or cool reception, you should persist in your attempts to keep communication open and interaction frequent. It's likely that later on you'll be very glad you did.

These relationships, when protected and nurtured, can be very rewarding for both yourself and your children. Frequently, in-laws really want to maintain their relationships but are not sure whether this will be welcomed or seen as appropriate. Their awkwardness and coolness are often simply confusion about how to act or relate to you now. With some warmth and reassurance they will often be relieved and very grateful that you want to remain connected and will gladly reciprocate.

## DEVELOPING NEW SOCIAL TIES FOR YOURSELF

Chances are, when you first began considering a separation, you started to think about making new friends or expanding your social network. However, this task may have become lost in the stress of the divorce. Now that you are divorced and worried about your children's adjustment, it may be even harder to push yourself into new social situations. You may tell yourself; "The children need me more now." You may feel guilty going out to parties or on dates and leaving the children home with babysitters. Or you may tell yourself that it's been a long time since you socialized as a single person and you're just not sure you can handle it.

*These are dangerous feelings.* Social isolation following a divorce can be harmful for you and your children. The tendency of many postdivorce parents is to throw themselves into parenting, often due to guilt, to "make up for what the children have lost." Some parents will allow a child, often the oldest, to become what therapists call a "parentified" child or to take on an inappropriate, adult role in the family. This child is given extra responsibilities, duties, and expectations. Sometimes these are in the form of caring for younger siblings. Even more damaging is when a child is allowed to substitute in other ways for the former spouse or to take on that spouse's role.

Some parents who are struggling with adjusting to the divorce and to being single will begin to rely on this "parentified" child for support and even nurturance. They will talk to the child as if they were peers. This can create highly dysfunctional responses in the children, ranging from overprotectiveness of the parent to depression and suicidal thoughts. It often strips them of their childhood and their growing-up experiences and overburdens their own adjustment to the divorce.

As an adult you must begin to go on with your life! Push yourself to go out with friends from work. Call friends you may not have heard from since your single days and try to reconnect. Take up new leisure activities such as bowling or tennis where you can meet new people. Join community or civic organizations or become more active in your religious community. Many churches or synagogues have their own groups or classes just for single individuals.

You may think, "I just don't feel like it yet." And you really don't! But it's important that you force yourself to do these things even when—especially when—you don't feel like it. It's a strange thing about feelings: often behaving as if you are feeling a certain way can actually lead to feeling that way. So, if necessary, pretend you are healing, that you are able to laugh again and socialize and enjoy new experiences. You may surprise yourself by *really* feeling better. After a while you can stop pretending and start living again.

The other danger to avoid is throwing yourself prematurely into a serious romantic relationship. This usually occurs simply as a way to fill the vacuum created by the divorce. Often these relationships are based on the need for social contact and companionship. But the urge to find a romantic partner is often great. There's often an expectation of adventure or for a magical rescuer. The drama of new sexual experiences can also become a test of your continuing attractiveness or prowess.

These are the transitional relationships that we mentioned in Chapter One. They provide you with a bridge into the new world of being single. They can help with your needs for adult interaction and companionship. They provide new information about yourself in social and romantic relationships. But they will not necessarily become permanent relationships. In fact during the first year after your divorce it may be dangerous for you to even imagine finding a permanent partner.

Remember: you need to be healthy and functioning in order to provide healthy and functional parenting for your children. As you make progress in your own adjustment, you will do better as a co-parent managing your new household.

## Tasks for Developing New Social Ties

1. Take time to heal emotionally.

2. Try to understand why your marriage failed.

3. Be alone with yourself; get to know yourself better before you find a new partner.

4. Set some new goals and priorities for yourself.

5. Don't assume that you need to remarry right away.

6. Build a new social network with people you enjoy.

7. Consider new educational or career directions.

8. Take up new sports or civic or religious activities.

9. Take your time getting into dating or new sexual experiences.

10. Seek some therapy or support groups if you need help in any of these areas.

11. Call on parents or other family members for support but don't rely on them exclusively.

12. Support and protect your children but don't rely on them to meet your own emotional needs.

13. Read as much as possible about the effects of divorce on children and adults and learn what you need to know to rebuild a stronger, happier life for yourself and for your children.

# *8*

# Starting a New Life:
# When Remarriage Occurs

SOME PEOPLE BELIEVE that a single piece of paper granting a divorce will magically transform their lives and make all the awful divorce "stuff"—the doubts, worries, confusions, upheavals—disappear. Unfortunately, there are actually two divorces that people need to get: a legal divorce and an emotional divorce.

Although the legal part of divorce may be over with that little piece of paper, the emotional divorce can be much trickier to accomplish. Some people are emotionally divorced before they even physically separate. Others may take decades to really feel disconnected from their former spouse emotionally; sadly, some never achieve it.

When couples become emotionally divorced, they are neither hateful nor loving with each other. Hate and love are continuing elements of intense connectedness. When people are emotionally divorced, their feelings are within a range between indifferent and casually caring. They may not wish the former spouses any ill will but they are no longer especially interested in what they are doing, whom they are with, or what is going on in their life except as those issues may, in some way, affect their children. They are happy for their good fortune, mildly concerned about their bad fortune, but truly disconnected. They have gone on with their lives and left their regrets as dim memories.

## DISCOVERING A
## NEW SELF

Getting to this place doesn't automatically happen when the divorce decree is issued. For many people it's a long uphill battle. The average length of time for adults to achieve an emotional divorce is one to two years after the legal decree. Often, the decree marks the beginning to being able to reach the end. It is a signal that you are now free to pursue a new path in your life, to be truly single, to have an abundance of opportunities and choices in front of you. Some find this exhilarating. Many find it terrifying. Most alternate between these feelings from day to day, until the days of hope and enthusiasm slowly begin to outnumber the days of numbing panic and fear.

Most people go through careful soul searching and analyzing during this process. They may do this alone at odd times of the day and night. They may use their closest friends to help them in this reconstruction process, to help them understand who they are, who they were, or who they should be. Many go to therapists to help them see into the mirror of their thoughts and feelings and firm up their tender new reconstructions of self. This can be a wonderful, horrible, painful, pleasurable process.

We tell our clients that while this self-reconstruction process is proceeding, social relationships should be kept casual and oriented toward fun and friendship. Date and enjoy some opposite-sex friendships. But don't get seriously involved with someone before you've truly obtained your emotional divorce. A new romance may feel good at first but you're delaying the healing process and stunting your possible new growth if you allow this to happen. You are also very likely to repeat the same mistakes you made previously and end with another divorce. (The incidence of second and third divorces is much higher than the incidence of first divorce.)

So how do you begin this process? First of all, you must begin to *enjoy* being alone. If you have been accustomed to many years of constant togetherness, even if it often consisted of hostility and pain, even the thought of being alone can be terrifying. But solitude can present many opportunities for self-reflection and self-discovery.

So take some time to learn about yourself—what you like or don't like, what brings you peace, what gives you joy. Begin to experience who you are, away from everybody else's experience of who you are. And ask these questions of yourself:

1. What were all the factors that contributed to our marriage failing? (Baggage from the families we grew up in; baggage from previous relationships; stresses of parents, in-laws, children, health, finances, jobs, friends; our personal limitations and liabilities; anger, dependency, possessiveness, intimacy problems; other factors such as . . .)

2. What do I really want from a committed, long-term relationship?

3. What changes do I need to make to achieve that type of relationship?

4. What type of partner do I need to achieve that type of relationship?

5. What can I do about my personal limitations and liabilities to change them to strengths and resources?

Getting to know yourself may be hard at first. The solitude may bring up painful, lonely, sad memories. But don't run away from them. Don't deny them or be frightened. Remember that you are alone—you can cry, scream, have a tantrum, pound your bed, say anything you like, and only you will know.

Give yourself an evening or two a week of wallowing in self-pity. On these designated evenings force yourself to feel as sorry for yourself as possible. Look at photographs and mementos, remember cherished times, and lament your awful fate. And when the time for self-pity is over and you've used up all the tears, begin the reconstruction process.

A plant cannot put out fresh shoots in new directions until the old branches are pruned back. People cannot grow until they divest themselves of the burden of guilt, failure, and regrets and look away from the past. If you can't complete this process through self-reflection or with your friends, seek out a family therapist to be your guide and coach through this surprising journey of self-discovery. You will be very glad that you gave yourself this wonderful gift.

## STAGE 12
## WHEN ONE PARENT
## DECIDES TO REMARRY

The first decision to remarry can produce a family crisis of cata-clysmic proportions. No matter how successfully everyone has adjust-ed after the divorce and no matter how long it has been since the divorce was final, the first remarriage can create an often unexpected and intense disruption.

We talked earlier about how family systems have a way of balancing themselves in order to function. Even after a divorce, a new dual sys-tem is created: you and the children, and your former spouse and the children. This new system develops its own sense of balance. After a while you and the children know what to expect in both of these sin-gle-parent systems. Over time the children learn to accommodate to your household and its routine just as they begin to accommodate to similar patterns in the other household.

When one of you becomes seriously involved with a new partner and begins to talk about remarriage, however, the rest of the family may begin to see this new player as a threat. Part of this reaction is because this new person creates an imbalance for the entire dual sys-tem, and now everyone must accommodate differently. And if a new significant person appears too soon after the divorce, the threat is even greater because everyone has only recently regained some new security and stability and no one wants to lose this so soon.

Children may see a stepparent as not only an intrusion into their security but as someone who'll take away their parent's time and atten-tion. Even worse, the new person may try to be another parent to them, which they would not welcome.

But the most dramatic reaction often comes from the spouse who is not remarrying. The strength of this reaction can be a clear measure of how much separation and letting go of the former marriage this other spouse has actually achieved. The responses can range from volatile threats to serious depression. Often, these reactions come as real sur-prises to both ex-spouses.

One wife, two years after the divorce, had become rather secure in her former husband's newly developed postdivorce role, even to the point where he was helping with mechanical problems around her house and doing yardwork. When he told her he was remarrying, she threatened to take him back to court to remove the joint custody ruling and vowed, "I will never let another woman be a parent to my children!"

In another case, five years after a divorce the wife had not adjusted well, was still isolated socially, and continued to fantasize that her husband would come back. When he announced his impending remarriage, she took an overdose of sleeping pills.

It's important to understand what this event of remarriage means in the family. The first remarriage seems to trigger two kinds of responses from the nonmarrying spouse. If he has not let go of the former relationship, the remarriage represents a sense of permanent loss. He feels replaced and unwanted. He may begin to fantasize that the new partner is getting more from his former wife than he himself received over the years of the marriage. Jealousy and possessiveness can be revived even many years after the divorce.

And a parent who has substituted overprotective involvement with her children for a healthy, adult social life can feel threatened that she is going to be supplanted by a new parent. She fears that this new adult might be a better parent or that the children might like her better. The fear of being replaced can lead to extreme panic and generalized anxiety for both men and women.

Two years after her divorce, one mother of three children hired an attorney and a private detective to dig up whatever they could find on her husband's new wife. She was preparing to file for a modification of custody to change their original agreement from joint to sole. She spent $10,000 trying to make a case that the new stepmother was unfit so she could restrict the father's access to the children. She never found any grounds for going back to court. In fact, she tried so hard to turn the children against the stepmother that they actually requested more time in their father's household. It took nearly a year of family therapy to repair the damage she had done to her relationship with her children by her jealousy and anxiety.

In another case, four years after the divorce and two thousand miles away from his former partner, one man became obsessed with her sexual activities with her new husband. Rationally, he remembered that during their marriage he was bored with their sexual relationship and often accused his wife of being frigid. Yet now he imagined she had become his ideal sexual partner and another man was enjoying it.

Not everyone's reactions are quite as intense. But it's important to recognize the potential for disruptions here. Even reasonable, well-adjusted spouses who have moved on with their lives will still feel a tinge of remorse or regret when their former spouse remarries. Sometimes they say, "These sad (or angry) feelings really surprised me. I thought I was over all that. I had trouble sleeping and felt nervous and agitated for a week after they got married."

If you expect this experience or feel it developing, you may want to attend some support groups or consult a therapist. The issue here is that these feelings are normal and predictable, not "bad" or "wrong." But you need to take care of them yourself. They cannot be imposed on your children or directed at either your former spouse or the new stepparent or partner.

## TELLING YOUR CHILDREN ABOUT YOUR PLANS TO REMARRY

Your children should be the first to hear of your plans to remarry, and they should hear it from you. Learning about it from someone else can create some angry interactions. Tell the children by yourself, not with your fiancé or other family members present. This can be a time for sharing important feelings and fears, which will be harder if someone else is there.

Also make sure that you, not the children, are the one to tell your former spouse. As soon as you've finished your initial discussion with the children, let your former spouse know right away. It shouldn't be the children's role to tell the other parent.

Ideally, by the time you tell them the news, the children will have already developed a solid, comfortable relationship with your new partner and the marriage will seem exciting. Don't be surprised, however, if they express mixed feelings about your decision. Any negative feelings probably have very little to do with not liking the new person. More typically they reflect fear of the unknown, anxiety about new changes, and leftover feelings of loyalty for their other parent and the former family system. The new marriage also means they must finally give up their fantasy of the family getting back together again some-day, and this may require some grieving and new adjustments.

Try to encourage the children to express *all* of their feelings—fears, anxieties, joys, and sorrows. You're asking them to make another huge adjustment. Be sensitive to the time they'll need to process this and accept it. Don't rush them. And don't attempt to force a certain type of response by saying, "Gee, I thought you'd be happy I was marrying Karen. I thought you liked her. Why the sad face?"

## STAGE 13
## WHEN THE SECOND
## PARENT REMARRIES

If your former spouse has remarried and you have been through the issues we identified in stage 12, there will be increasing pressures for you to remarry too. These pressures may come from your children, who either feel sorry for you or who want to have a new family like their other parent has created, or from your family and friends, who may see remarriage as a way of getting on with your life.

But the most serious pressure will come from within. After going through the feelings of replacement in stage 12, you may want what the other spouse has. Often there are feelings that "maybe something is wrong with me" since your former spouse has remarried and you haven't. You may imagine that remarrying will take away your fears of losing the children to the new stepparent.

Behind all of these feelings and pressures is an intuitive sense that a serious imbalance exists. While this is usually unspoken, it seems painfully clear to you that your former wife has recreated a shiny new family system to replace the old one lost in divorce. She seems to be going on with her life. She has a new lover and companion while you sit at home with rented videos or cruise the social scene hoping some-one magical will appear. Your secret fears of stage 12 are coming true: the children seem to like being with that new family even though they're still uncomfortable with the new stepparent. You could hardly listen to them tell you about their family trip to the Grand Canyon and how much fun they had taking care of their new baby sister.

You begin to imagine how nice it would be to have some companionship again. You want to provide your own shiny new family system for your children. You imagine trips you could take together again as a family. You decide that you can't go through the holidays without having a family with you.

Take your time! Resist these pressures! We have seen too many individuals jump into remarriage prematurely because of these feelings. To remarry simply to rebalance the system is one of the unhealthiest steps you can take. The odds of finding a suitable partner under these circumstances are very low.

Step back from these feelings and pressures; try to regain your objectivity. Remember some of the predivorce fantasies you had about being on your own, traveling, going back to school, taking tennis lessons, dating exciting new partners. You don't have to give up on those just because your former spouse has remarried.

It *is* possible to create a successful single-parent family system on your own. The children will not be damaged if they have only one stepparent instead of two. In fact they'll be much happier if their single parent is healthy and functioning well. They do not need another parent embroiled in marital conflict and potential divorce again.

## UNDERSTANDING CHILDREN'S VIEWS ON REMARRIAGE

After one parent has remarried, many children will pressure their other parent to remarry. This is because they will worry about you being on your own and lonely. They may have seen you crying late at night. They will often make it their mission to find you a new mate and begin scouting around for potential parents from your opposite-sex friends.

Other children may respond in just the opposite manner by encouraging you to stay single and resisting all your efforts to introduce them to your dates. These children may be assuming the "parentified" role that we discussed earlier. Their mission may be to replace their other parent and become your protector and manager. They may feel it is their responsibility to become your "adult" partner from whom you can get support and in whom you can confide. Such children will actually give up their own friends and activities to play this role for you.

This can be a tempting and seductive role for single parents who are lonely and discouraged. Without thinking, they can begin to respond to a child offering emotional support and companionship. Allowing this kind of pattern to develop, however, can be very unhealthy for you and your child. Children who gain this power with a parent do not give it up easily when you do eventually find a new mate.

A dramatic example involved Jason, a big, burly fifteen-year-old who used athletics to work out his frustrations over the divorce. He had become a state champion high school wrestler. He had also become his mother's protector over the three years since the divorce. The mother, Marie, was lonely and sad, and had developed no adult social life since the divorce. Jason had become so involved with his mother that he visited his father and stepmother less and less. He even broke up with his girlfriend when she pressured him for more time and kidded him about being too involved with his mother.

A predictable crisis occurred. Frank, a co-worker, began asking Marie out. She turned him down for several months but then decided to accept. While she was in the house preparing for the date Jason met Frank on the front porch and told him his mother had become very sick and couldn't go out with him that night. (Does this sound like your parent when you were fourteen years old?)

Frank assumed this must be true since Jason seemed so sincere, and he left. But Jason never told his mother that Frank had come. Marie was devastated, presuming she'd been stood up. Jason was there, of course, to comfort her. And it wasn't until Monday morning that she learned what had really happened. While she was furious with Jason, she'd come to rely on him too much to punish him. When she later returned from another date with Frank, Jason and two of his friends were waiting on the front porch with baseball bats. Marie had lost control of Jason and Frank never returned.

Another case involved a thirteen-year-old girl who had become the caretaker, housekeeper, and confidant to her single dad. She tolerated his casual dating, but as he became more serious about one woman she escalated her efforts to break them up. First she told lies about seeing this woman with another man at the mall. Then she had stomach cramps and was even able to make herself throw up before their dates, convincing the father to stay home with her. One weekend, when she was with her mother but knew her father was out of town with this woman, she took an overdose of mixed pills from her mother's medicine cabinet and had to be rushed to the hospital. Of course the father was called home. This was an act of manipulation, not attempted suicide.

These illustrations demonstrate the importance of maintaining boundaries for yourself as a single parent and not allowing your children to become your caretaker or confidant. Encourage them to be active with their friends and to participate in activities away from home. Make it clear to them that you can be fine when they are gone, that you have your own friends and pursuits. They need to continue to be carefree children without adult worries and responsibilities.

The decision to remarry represents an important step in going on with your life. But it also creates new challenges for your children and former spouse. Take your time and try to prepare everyone. If it's your former spouse who is remarrying first, step back and be reasonable; watch for your own feelings of disappointment or of losing the chance to reconcile. Be careful not to feel pressured into remarrying prematurely yourself.

# 9

# Living in a Blended Family Network

THE FINAL STAGE in the divorce process involves creating a new family system. These are often called stepfamilies, but we prefer the term blended families. "Step" implies that someone doesn't fit or belong, that someone is "out of step."

When two parents remarry, and both have been previously married and divorced, they bring with them not only children from their prior marriages but also members of their families of origin and even former spouses who are still parents for the children. The task of forming this new family system is truly a process of blending many individuals and roles from the other systems into one network.

This is a very complex process. Compare this task of trying to integrate and manage the members of several systems with the relative simplicity of your first marriage. Then it was only you and your new partner with perhaps some influence from your parents. Now you have new in-laws and old in-laws, plus your new wife's former husband and their three children, not to mention your former wife's new husband and his kids with their grandmother living with them.

In this final stage we present a model to help you understand the various parts of a blended family so you can be more objective and know what to expect. We help you identify a healthy path through the complexity of blended family experiences and understand them in the context of the larger network.

## STAGE 14
## FORMING A
## BLENDED FAMILY

The struggles you may recall when you and your former spouse were still single parents may seem insignificant when compared to the tasks of blending families together in a healthy manner after both of you have remarried.

First let's take a moment to look at Figure 9.1. We have drawn a genogram to present a picture of all the possible family systems that may be involved when both of you remarry. A genogram is simply a diagram using squares and circles to show where each member of the family fits. You may want to count: there are a total of nine possible systems! This is why we believe it's more realistic to refer to it as a network of family systems.

If you study this picture a little you'll be able to substitute the players in your particular situation. This is important, since to achieve a healthy blending of family systems you need to provide structure, organization, and clarity of roles not only for the children but for the adults too.

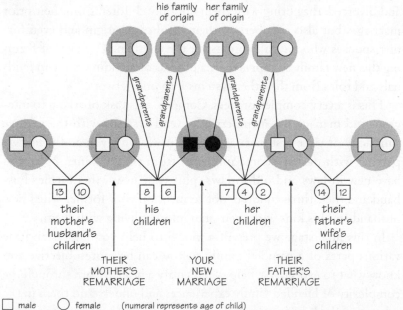

Figure 9.1 The Blended Family Network

There are four central aspects to understanding blended families that we think will help you anticipate and recognize potential problem areas for yourself: the various subsystems, the boundaries, the parents, and the interactive pattern.

### Dimensions of a Blended Family System

1. Subsystems: who are the players and where do they fit?

2. Boundaries: who are the adults and who are the children?

3. The roles of parents: issues of authority and discipline.

4. Interaction between the blended systems: issues of access, communication, and loyalties.

## DEFINING THE SUBSYSTEMS

Every family system has the potential for four interacting groups of relationships called subsystems (see Figure 9.2).

I. The spousal subsystem

2. The sibling subsystem

3. The parent-child subsystem

4. The intergenerational subsystem

### The Spousal Subsystem.

This subsystem consists of the husband and wife. It is the one subsystem that is dissolved in divorce. The other subsystems will be altered but will continue to function. In a blended family, a new subsystem of husband and wife is formed to replace the former ones, which perhaps for both spouses ended in divorce. This new relationship has many more challenges and difficulties to face than the spousal relationships formed in the first marriages.

A remarried couple, where possibly both partners have children, does not have the luxury of several years to get to know each other without children present or without the complications of former spouses. This new relationship is always shadowed, at least in the first

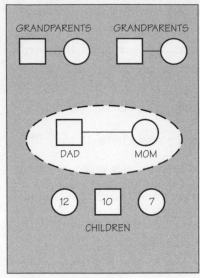

1. Spousal Subsystem

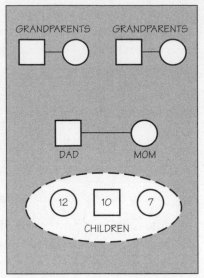

2. Sibling Subsystem

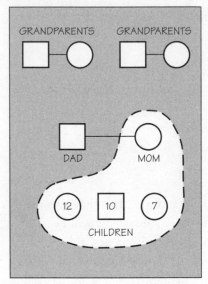

3. Parent-Child Subsystem

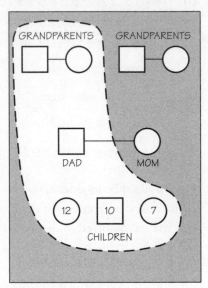

4. Intergenerational Subsystem

Figure 9.2. Subsystems in the Family.

several years, by these former marriages. There are issues of visitation and access. There are co-parenting decisions to be made. There is the question of child support and perhaps spousal maintenance. Over the years, the most common problem that we have encountered in blended families is the failure of the remarried couple to define and protect their relationship from these other influences.

To achieve a healthy blended family network, it's imperative that you and your new spouse create a sense of bonding, intimacy, and privacy for yourselves. This is no easy task. Both of you will be at the mercy of intrusions from children, stepchildren, former spouses, and family-of-origin members. You may feel guilty taking time for yourselves, telling the children to stay home while you go out to dinner together, taking a vacation without the children, and being firm with former spouses who are intrusive or who want to change the access schedule at the last minute. This guilt may be left over from the divorce and feelings that you do not want to "hurt" the children any further. One of the best ways to protect your new marital relationship is to define boundaries around it. (We'll discuss these further in the next section.)

**The first task in developing a healthy blended family system is to protect and nurture your new marital relationship!**

### The Sibling Subsystem.
This includes all the children in the family. In a blended family this may involve "his" children and "her" children. So if you started with two children in your marriage that just ended and remarried someone with two children from his first marriage, you now have a sibling subsystem of four. These children could conceivably range in age from one to fifteen. To make it more difficult, they might not even know each other. And they certainly don't want any more competition for their role in the family or for their parent's attention.

From the children's perspective this new sibling subsystem may be even more complex. Not only do they have to get to know new stepsiblings from your spouse's former marriage, but they may also have new stepsiblings from their other parent's new spouse's former marriage. So if you take all of the normal interactional sibling rivalries, competitions, and jealousies that you experienced with your own children before the divorce and magnify them among many siblings, who may not even want to live together and have not yet accepted you as a new adult in their lives, you can begin to see why blended family life can seem so difficult and confusing for everyone.

We worked with one six-year-old boy whose mother had remarried a man with four children aged eleven to eighteen. The boy was overwhelmed by all these new, bigger, louder stepsiblings. He followed his mother around like a puppy and cried when she left for work. It took nearly six months for him to accept and trust the new stepsiblings and for them to learn how to relate to him as a little brother. It is often easier for older children to accept younger stepsiblings than young ones to accept older ones. It feels a lot like being bumped down in the family pecking order.

### The Parent-Child Subsystem.

This is the most complex of the four because it involves the interaction of the spousal subsystem (the adults) and the sibling subsystem (all the children). Whatever successes you may have had as a parent before your divorce or even as a single parent will be dramatically tested in the blended family experience. The basic rules are the same: the adults are supposed to be the parents, the children are supposed to behave as children and not adults, the adults are supposed to behave as adults and not children, and the parents are supposed to be in charge of the family.

However, the parents' life in a blended family is much more complicated. You continue to be the parent of your children, but you also inherit parenting duties of your spouse's children. In your prior marriage your children were with you all the time. Now you have several other children who alternate weeks in your household. On top of that, these children barely know you and often don't accept you as a parent in their lives. Furthermore you have to continue to build a healthy coparenting relationship with your former spouse while perhaps at the same time dealing with the former spouse of your new mate. Not to mention the new spouse of your former mate.

All these are just the external issues as you and your new spouse must develop your own co-parenting relationship with all these children. Try not to feel overwhelmed; there are healthy ways to pull all this together.

From the children's perspective, life with twice the "normal" number of parents and a variety of kids they never grew up with—some their own age, some many years older or younger—is a confusing, chaotic series of emotional adjustments. Jealousy, envy, possessiveness of parents and belongings, grief, and anger all begin to create behavioral adjustments, both good and bad. Roles that the child was used to in the former family system—being the eldest, the baby, the hero—all require adjustment and modification.

Children cannot occupy their same former roles in new blended families. There can be only one oldest and one youngest. If one child's accustomed role has been taken over by a new stepsibling, there is a period of time where she has to learn new behaviors and adjust to new expectations. It's easy to put yourself in your children's shoes. Imagine you were ten and the eldest in your family; you probably were treated with some respect by your six- and four-year-old siblings. Perhaps your parents had sometimes given you the responsibility of taking care of them. Now imagine you are put into a blended family with sixteen- and fourteen-year-old stepsisters and they are given the responsibility of taking care of you. You may very well become frustrated, angry, and discouraged.

Some children become temporarily depressed during this adaptation period; some become continually angry. Some children may regress to a younger age emotionally and become overly dependent or anxious. Others may choose to distance themselves from the new family by spending more time with friends. All of these are adaptations to the dramatic changes the children are experiencing, some of them more helpful than others. Their purpose is to give a child time to adjust to the fluctuations and uncertainties of this unfamiliar world of the blended family.

During the initial phase of adaptation, many children will complain to their other biological parent about all the changes and new people in this new family system that they find unfamiliar and uncomfortable. They will often show far more distress in their other home to their other parent than in the blended family to which they are trying to adapt. They do this because the new system will feel unfamiliar and a little intimidating. They are not sure where they stand or how their complaints will be heard or dealt with. It is also a way to show loyalty and commitment to the other parent, as if to say, "You don't have to feel bad about them being together; all kinds of lousy things are happening over there." Usually it will take six to twelve months for the emotional upheaval to settle and for children to find the right niche for themselves. They may still grumble and fuss occasionally but will probably have returned to their prior levels of emotional functioning after a year.

If the children still appear unusually distressed after the first year, or if their distress becomes so intense that it really affects their everyday functioning, then you need to have the situation evaluated by a child or family therapist. Often just the opportunity for a child to talk to someone "safe" outside the family about their conflicting feelings can provide great relief. If the adjustment problems are more serious, then the blended family can benefit from all working together with a family therapist.

### The Intergenerational Subsystem.

This defines everyone's own ties and roles with their families of origin. The powerful influence of this subsystem is often overlooked by families and therapists alike. Adults' relationships with their parents and siblings and the children's relationships with their grandparents, aunts, and uncles provide an important backdrop for all families. For blended families, this subsystem can become a healthy and meaningful resource or a disruptive and intrusive problem.

Often grandparents have been involved in supporting their adult children financially, sometimes paying the attorney bills in custody disputes, to protect their daughter's or son's control of their grandchildren. Sometimes these older parents encouraged the divorce, saying they never liked their son- or daughter-in-law. Other parents may have tried to forbid the divorce saying it brought shame to their family. None of these experiences with your family of origin is going to make it easy for you to introduce new individuals into your life or the lives of their grandchildren.

On the other hand, it's important to protect your children's relationships with and access to all their grandparents. Grandparents can become important emotional resources and stabilizing influences on children during and after a divorce. It's also important to help grandparents realize how destructive they can be by continuing to take sides after the divorce is over. We hear many stories from children who give up on relationships with their grandparents because every time they go to visit the grandparents tell them how much of a jerk their other parent is and if she or he hadn't done this or that their parents would still be together.

We are great fans of grandparents who have been able to stay out of the divorce battle and remain healthy and objective in their relationships with their grandchildren. Grandparents can provide an important sense of continuity to children. They are the carriers of the family history and can help children to remember their roots and their ties to their family system. This can be important when the rest of their family seems to be coming apart.

Most grandparents do not have as intense reactions to the divorce as the children experience from you and your former spouse. Therefore it can feel "safer" to the children to discuss these memories and feelings with them. Grandparents often become a safe haven when children are caught in the crossfire of difficult divorces and can help the children explore their feelings and questions with a degree of calm and trust. When children are in the middle of struggling with the divorce or adapting to a new blended family, we often recommend a brief visit or even a vacation with their grandparents to provide a settling experience for them.

One shy, quiet little seven-year-old girl we know began to call her grandparents, who lived in another state, about twice a week. They were neutral and supportive and gave her a sense of relief from the confusion of her mother's new marriage. They also provided an important link to her memories of the former family. We encouraged the parents to allow her to continue this for a while because it became a therapeutic experience for her.

Stepgrandparents can also play a significant role for children. Typically children do not become as attached to their new stepgrandparents as they have to their biological ones, but they can be confused or hurt if these new grandparents seem to neglect or reject them. If their stepsiblings are lavishly remembered on birthdays or holidays by their own biological grandparents while they themselves are ignored, feelings of resentment can occur. This can become translated into jealousies and rivalries among the entire sibling subsystem in the blended family. It can also create major conflicts and resentments between the remarried couple and even the former marital partners.

One twelve-year-old girl in our practice became angry and aggressive toward her two new and younger stepsiblings following their first Christmas holiday together, even though she had been very loving with them before that. Several weeks later she revealed to her father that she was hurt and disappointed because the stepsiblings received twice as many gifts from their grandparents as she received in total from everyone in her family. This led to two months of conflict between her dad and his new wife before they requested some help.

This is an example of a situation where you and your new partner need to take control as parents and establish some clear limits and boundaries. It's not realistic to expect all the children to be treated equally, but you need to avoid huge and noticeable differences between how one set of children is treated as compared to the other. This goes back to maintaining a sense of balance and clear roles in your new blended family.

How do you exert some influence over this complex blended family network of new spouses, new children, new in-laws, and new former spouses? Is it really possible to turn this into a healthy, functioning family system? We believe one of the keys to this task is learning how to develop clear boundaries.

**The second most important task in developing a healthy blended family system is to define clear boundaries!**

## DEFINING BOUNDARIES

Once you have recognized who all the new people are and more or less where they're supposed to fit, the task of defining boundaries becomes clearer.

Boundaries represent invisible lines that mark where people fit within a family system. They define distinctions between the generations, subsystems, and roles that everyone plays in a family. It's somewhat like a wild animal urinating on a tree to mark its territory. Perhaps it's not quite as dramatic in human families, but such boundaries lets others know where they and their family belong and where others do not.

For example, a mother may have to challenge the intrusions by her new in-laws into her own parenting and lifestyle. In one family the in-laws arrived for a week-long visit just three months after their son had remarried. Both the son and his new wife had a young child from previous marriages. Firmer boundaries might have helped the husband to say to his parents, "We would enjoy seeing you but give us another few months to get settled and organized." Unfortunately, he was afraid this might hurt their feelings, and so he said nothing.

When the parents arrived they proceeded to criticize the new wife's housekeeping, her parenting of not only their grandson but her own daughter, and her cooking. They didn't believe in divorce and were uncomfortable with this remarriage. The husband never intervened to set boundaries or to protect his new wife. As a result this one intrusive visit created an underlying conflict for this couple that lasted until they entered marital therapy six years later.

Boundaries create protection for parts of the family system as well as defining roles of authority and responsibility. A blended family system without clear and firm boundaries will turn into chaos and a continual struggle for control among its members. Boundaries need to be clear but also flexible. They need to be able to protect the members but also be open enough to let in new people and new information.

We show the different shapes that boundaries take in Figure 9.3. Diffuse boundaries are too thin; they don't really protect the members inside. Closed boundaries are too rigid; they will reduce the communication and interaction with outside members. Open boundaries are the best; they can be clear and firm when necessary, yet also flexible and open to let others in or out.

### Boundaries for the Marriage.

Let's go back to your first task: protecting and nurturing your new marital relationship. Think about what kind of boundaries you had in your former marriage. Were your parents often telling you how to raise your children and manage your family? Did your children burst into your bedroom without knocking? Were you uncomfortable clos-

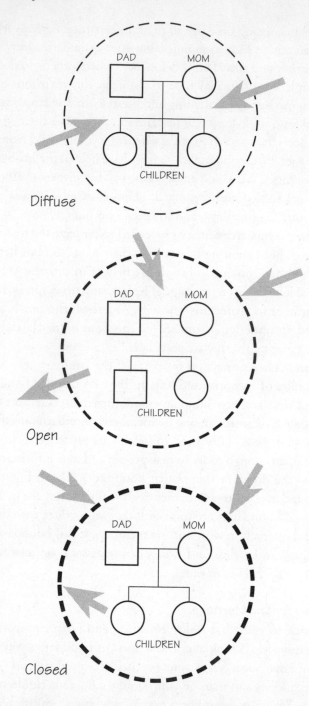

Figure 9.3. Types of Family Boundaries.

ing your children's or your own bedroom doors because you could not hear them? If you answered yes to any of these questions you probably had fairly diffuse boundaries around your marriage. You'll have to work hard in your new blended family for the next few years to establish more effective boundaries.

Without clear and firm boundaries to protect some privacy for yourselves, your new relationship will be open to the intrusions from parents, children, stepchildren, new in-laws, former spouses, former in-laws, and on and on. Defining these boundaries will help you regain a sense of control and direction for your blended family.

Many blended families become what therapists refer to as child-focused families; the children's needs and activities are given the highest priorities, even over the needs of the new spouses. Many divorced parents carry a lot of guilt about their children, and this guilt becomes translated into attending to every need of their children while discounting or sacrificing their own needs.

Children who grow up in child-focused families are spoiled with attention and learn few limits on their behaviors. As teenagers they often don't know how to respect limits set by other adults and have little sense of boundaries for themselves or their own relationships. Such children are frequently troubled adolescents who have a great deal of difficulty being responsible and learning self-discipline and self-control. As adults, these problems can plague their relationships and lead to dysfunctional patterns throughout their life.

### Children Need Boundaries Too.

Children need to learn to respect other people's privacy, physical boundaries, and property—and this is best learned in the family. Rules that may have been relaxed or nonexistent in your former family need to be defined clearly and enforced in your new blended family.

For example, bathroom doors need to be closed to teach children privacy about their bodies. Parents need to insist upon appropriate levels of dress for all members of the family. This is especially true in blended families, where anxieties may occur about the physical appearance and development of older stepsiblings or where concerns about incest or molestation may be present. The casualness of your former household needs to be reexamined. Your twelve-year-old daughter may have been comfortable walking around the house in her

### How to Define Boundaries

1. Close your bedroom door at night. If the children are old enough, encourage them to close theirs as well.

2. Define your bedroom as a private place, not just for sexual reasons but for your own adult space and time to communicate with your new spouse.

3. Firmly cut off intrusions by your children or the stepchildren into your personal activities or the interactions between you and your spouse.

4. Do not let your child sit in the front seat of the car when you drive while your new spouse sits in the back.

5. Don't let a child sit between you and your spouse on the couch or when you go to the movies or sit together on other occasions. Don't miss the symbolic messages in this behavior.

6. Do not let your own parents or your new in-laws call too frequently to check up on whether you are really taking good care of their grandchildren.

7. Don't tolerate your own parents or other relatives criticizing your former or new spouse in front of you or your children.

bra and panties in your prior family; her younger siblings probably ignored her. But to do this in front of her new eleven- and fourteen-year-old stepsiblings would be inappropriate. Children in blended families also need to learn new rules about borrowing clothing and other possessions of their new stepsiblings and stepparent.

Many children in a new blended family who grew up with few rules or boundaries will have difficult lessons to learn about respecting others' personal space. This includes issues of touching or hitting, good or bad. Children must have the right to refuse touches they don't want.

These personal boundary issues are extremely important to developing a successfully blended family system. The mistake parents often make is assuming that the patterns of boundaries and privacy that existed in their former family will be appropriate or acceptable in their new blended family. Many biological families tend to have more diffuse and relaxed boundaries than may be necessary for the blended family.

As parents you will find that the time and effort it takes to attend to these boundaries for your children and yourself will be greatly rewarded in the smoother functioning of your family life. These boundaries will help to manage anxieties among the children and protect everyone's sense of self and identity. And of course you need to become effective models for these boundaries yourselves.

Here is an example of how we help blended families begin to recognize and work on their boundaries. We've found that the way people seat themselves at dinner often indicates the boundaries in that family. In most cases these positions don't change once they become established. So we ask families to describe how they arrange themselves around their dinner table.

In one family that we worked with, Mom and Dad sat at opposite ends of an oval table. Mom's two children sat side by side to her right. Dad's one child sat across from them on the other side of the table to Dad's right. This is often how child-focused families define their boundaries. It means that the children are the center of attention. Think about how this arrangement makes it impossible for Mom and Dad to carry on a private conversation, or even a casual one, with three children seated between them. It also shows that the process of blending the two sets of children is going slowly since they are separated across the table.

We suggested that Mom and Dad might have important things to talk about at dinner since they had not seen each other all day. We wondered out loud what it would be like if they sat together on one side of the table and the three children could arrange themselves however they wished around the rest of the table.

Patterns don't change easily. This blended family had been together for only about one year, yet it took three weeks before Mom and Dad ran out of excuses for why they couldn't change the seating arrangement, everything from "It would be harder to manage the children at the table" to "It would feel selfish if we were to talk to each other instead of the children."

When Mom and Dad finally began to like the idea, the children began to resist. They didn't want to change their seats. The younger of Mom's children, a six-year-old with a precocious vocabulary, actually cried in a session because she was afraid she wouldn't be able to sit next to her mother. Another child worried that the parents might get too "cozy" if they sat next to each other! Some of the not so subtle rivalries between the two sets of children became more apparent than the parents had ever realized.

After nearly four weeks of working on this, we finally asked the family to try a new seating arrangement the following week. When we saw the family the next week they all agreed it had been a disaster. The children fought with one another, cried, and one finally left the table. The problem here was that Mom and Dad had not developed clear and firm boundaries, and so they were unable to manage and control even this simple task of sitting together at dinner.

You may wonder why we would spend nearly five weeks of therapy on this one issue. It's because this simple task of sitting together reflects the roles and boundaries for the entire system. The conflicts that were played out over the seating issue were identical to those that occurred in a hundred different ways and times throughout a normal week.

After several weeks of struggling, these parents finally gained some control and were successful in maintaining these boundaries. The children settled down at dinner and actually learned some new ways to relate to one another. The parents liked the changes so much they set up a new tradition: one evening a week they fed the children early and had a private dinner at eight o'clock. They even went on a vacation without the children.

This exercise around the table was a practical way of helping all family members experience their relationships with one another from a new perspective and learn how to define their interactions in healthier ways.

**The third most important task in developing a healthy blended family system is to define clear roles of authority and control.**

## DEFINING THE ROLES OF PARENTS IN AUTHORITY AND DISCIPLINE

If you remember the family system in Figure 9.1, there were potentially three dads and three moms involved across the immediate blended family network. That means that not only must you and your new spouse deal with the two sets of children in the context of your new household, but you also will have to deal with the children's other natural parents and their remarried spouses and even the children from the other marriage. To blend this into a healthy working system calls for a program that makes clear who is in charge when and where, and what role both the remarried and natural parents will play.

There are usually two effective but different patterns of defining authority in a blended family:

1. Each natural parent retains primary authority over her or his own children and consults with the new spouse about parenting issues.

2. Both remarried parents share authority over all the children and co-parent as a team.

There are pros and cons to both approaches. Your choice will depend on the ages of the children, the number of children involved, the parenting role of your new spouse, and the length of time the new family has been together.

## DEFINING INTERACTION BETWEEN THE BLENDED SYSTEMS

As a remarried parent, you'll often feel like an air traffic controller, managing the comings and goings of numerous members of your new blended system. You may be called upon to coordinate child-related activities with your former spouse, your former spouse's new spouse, your former spouse's new spouse's former spouse, and sometimes even your former spouse's new spouse's children. To do this successfully will take a great deal of organization, objectivity, patience, and cooperation.

This is why we recommend that you take your time before you enter a new marriage. It's also why we emphasize the importance of disconnecting from the emotional hurts and anger of your former marriage. You cannot be expected to develop a healthy blended family if you are still at war with your former spouse or jealous of a new spouse.

The success of coordinating these interactions smoothly becomes another boundary issue. You need to be able to draw boundaries around your own new blended system, yet be able to adjust them when coordination and interactions are necessary. Here boundaries take on a more subtle role of essentially everyone minding their own business. That may sound a little harsh but it is the bottom-line issue. For example, you may need to tell your former husband that the way you and your new husband are parenting the children is fine. You may need to tell him that the fact you put a telephone in your seventeen-year-old daughter's bedroom is none of his business. When he wants to change weekends you may need to say, "No, we already have plans made for that weekend." We always encourage communication and flexibility between former spouses, but the point here is that at times you need to set your boundaries firmly and protect the life of your new blended family.

For your own blended system to work smoothly, you and your spouse need to focus on your new lives together. You do not need to take time to comment on either former spouse's parenting style. You do not need to react with hurt or anger when you hear comments that you are being too strict or that you shouldn't have bought your stepdaughter a blouse that color. Simply pull your boundaries around your family a little tighter for a while until the others are able to go on with their own parenting.

We work with many blended families where people cannot stay out of one another's lives. In reality the main interaction that you need to have with the other family is sharing important information about health, education, or social concerns of the children and coordinating the logistics of their activities. The only serious exception to this would be if you genuinely believe that your former spouse or the new spouse is neglecting or abusing the children. But be careful about jumping to conclusions here. (We'll discuss children's manipulations in the next section.) If you have serious concerns about stories of abuse or neglect, talk to your former spouse first. If that doesn't work, take your children to a therapist who can evaluate what is going on. Of course, if you have evidence that the children are in immediate danger then you should report it immediately to either the police or the local child protective agency.

When your coordination efforts are continually frustrated or fail, it may be helpful to suggest that all the blended parents go to a family therapist together to work this out. You may be surprised how willing they may be. Try to find a family therapist who specializes in working with blended families. (The American Association for Marriage and Family Therapy, listed in Appendix B, may be of help here.) Not all therapists have been trained to work with large families and some may be reluctant to see you with your former spouse and their remarried spouse.

## RECOGNIZING CHILDREN'S MANIPULATIONS IN BLENDED FAMILIES

You need to be aware that children usually have their own issues and agendas in their adjustment process and that these issues may be very different from your own. Children will often hold on to the fantasy of reuniting their parents, especially if they have relationship difficulties with a new stepparent. This may lead them to try to undermine or even destroy your new relationship. They may attempt many ploys to get their parents reengaged in activities together, hoping or wishing that something magical will happen between them.

Children who need to reunite their parents may keep them stirred up by telling tales of the stepparent's "cruelty" or the "terrible" way they are being disciplined. Other children may get in trouble at school just to get their parents to deal with them together. For these children, their parents' anger—with each other or with them—is preferable to their parents being emotionally disconnected.

Because of jealousy issues or the loss of roles in their new blended system, children sometimes attempt manipulations regarding their stepsiblings. A child may try to get them in trouble, either to make them look bad or to gain more favor from a parent. This can occur because there are real or perceived differences in how the various children are disciplined.

Often, a newly remarried father may be gone all day at work, leaving the new stepmother in charge. Naturally, she can parent her own children more comfortably than his. And his children may resent her stepping into this parent role so quickly. So they may begin to behave horribly to demonstrate their resentment of the intrusion of this new parent into a role reserved for their biological parent. When father returns home that evening he is blasted by his new wife about how horrible "his" children are. He may get angry at them to support his wife, but they may become more angry in return and feel alienated from him, producing a new vicious cycle.

Often this scenario requires professional help to sort out the manipulative and destructive behaviors and create new patterns. Don't underestimate children's potential for creating difficulties when they are feeling abandoned, unloved, or unwanted! Such manipulations should be viewed as a child's way of trying to regain identity and equilibrium or find a sense of power and control, all of which were damaged by the divorce experience. Underneath these behaviors are your child's needs for nurturance, support, and understanding. If the children are only punished and their needs suppressed, many undesirable side effects can arise that can plague their development and the healthy functioning of the blended family for years.

For example, two years after his parents had divorced, a seven-year-old boy was having real trouble adjusting to the new man who had moved in with his mother. He'd made many subtle attempts to let the mother know that he did not want to share her with this intruder in his life. One day after returning from a visit with his father, he announced to the boyfriend: "My daddy said he is going to kill you one night if you keep living in our house. I've seen the new gun he has, too."

The mother overreacted by calling the police immediately without considering whether this was accurate or calling the father to clarify the story. She suspended the father's access to the boy even after he told her that he had never said anything like that. She was using this incident to get back at him for earlier issues in the divorce. By her impulsive overreaction, she created incredible guilt for the child.

The father was interviewed by the police and had to get an attorney to help him restore his access. When the attorneys asked us to evaluate the situation it had already been three months since the father had seen his son. It did not take very long for the boy to admit to Sandy that he had seen a TV show that had given him the idea to make up this story. He hoped it would scare the boyfriend into moving out of the house. He felt bad that he hadn't seen his dad in a long time and that he had caused so much trouble, but once the lie was told, the mother's strong reaction made it hard for him to back off his story or change it.

All the families that we've met in this chapter could have benefitted from better communication between the former spouses and clearer boundaries to protect the new blended system. Remember: the goals for completing a healthy divorce are to let go of your former relationship, establish boundaries to protect your new relationship and family system, and go on with your life!

# 10

## Epilogue: Returning to Janet's and Jim's Divorce

FINALLY, LET'S RETURN to Janet and Jim, the couple we met at the beginning of this book. We left them at a therapy session where Jim announced he'd been involved in an affair. In her anger, Janet made a number of threats and stormed out. Jim responded with his own threats. Fortunately, however, their attorneys encouraged Janet and Jim to return for several joint sessions to be clear about what they really wanted to do with their marriage.

Now we can look at their situation as a way of illustrating how they might have avoided this painful and angry confrontation and how the various stages of divorce that we've identified in the book helped them work through the process.

In our next session with Janet and Jim, we learned that he had begun to feel dissatisfied and unhappy in the marriage as long ago as six or seven years (this is stage I, the Clouds of Doubt). He had never looked at this very carefully, but as he talked Jim remembered mixed feelings about their third pregnancy. He felt that Janet pushed for this despite his concern about finances and a possible career move.

"I guess I lost Janet and my marriage to the pregnancy and all of the children," Jim said. "She was never a wife or lover, but always a parent. A couple of years after Andy was born she started to get depressed and just never interacted with me. I guess I secretly blamed the children and never felt I could say anything to Janet."

Janet was amazed at this revelation. At first she denied it, but after she thought about it she decided it could have been true. She was the eldest child in her family of origin. Her mother had been an alcoholic and she had been given the role of caretaking her younger brothers and often her own mother. "It just felt natural to involve myself with the children like I had done my whole life. And Jim never seemed to need me for anything, he was always healthy and busy at work. I never thought I could have been too involved with them."

In the next session Jim reported that in the following years he just pulled away more and more. He hadn't thought about other relationships then but simply involved himself in his work and took every opportunity to travel (stage 2, the Cold Shoulder). It was not until about a year ago, when his business was going very well and he felt more secure, that he started imagining relationships with other women (stage 3, Preseparation Fantasies).

He felt angry that he couldn't approach Janet for affection or sex, and that she always seemed so depressed and uninterested in him. He had seen a few women for drinks and dinner but never became involved with anyone until he met Linda about six months earlier. He found her engaging, stimulating, and sexually attractive, and as he said, "One thing led to another." He felt young and appreciated and no longer believed that he loved Janet.

Janet really struggled when she heard all this; she cried frequently during the sessions. Her early anger turned into recriminations against herself and pleading for Jim to stay in therapy and try to repair the marriage. Jim was reluctant but agreed to our suggestion of planning a couple of dates together just to see if any hope was still there. We always try to help couples slow down the divorce process, step back, and take a look at the bigger picture. Unfortunately for Janet's and Jim's relationship, the distance and silence through those early years deprived them of an opportunity to face problems, deal with them, and have a future.

In many respects, their inability to deal with each other—Jim's silence about his unhappiness and anger and Janet's depression and excessive involvement with the children—had doomed the marriage six or seven years earlier. We believe that if they had recognized these early warning signs and talked to each other or sought marital therapy even two years earlier, the marriage could have been saved. This is why we want you to recognize these early stages as red flags in your own relationship.

Jim returned the following week and reported that he just could not identify any loving feelings for Janet and that too much unhappy history was in the way of trying to repair the marriage. It was also clear that he was not willing to back off the new relationship with Linda. By this time Janet was a little more prepared for the finality of Jim's statement, but it would take her many months in therapy with Sandy to get control of her growing depression and begin to accept the divorce.

Our next role was to help them plan their separation (stage 4). Jim wanted to separate as soon as possible; in fact he had already put down a deposit on a small apartment across town. Janet became angry that he wanted to move out so quickly to be with his girlfriend. Again, we tried to help them slow down and look at what they needed and what would be best for their children.

We helped Jim see that having a tiny apartment across town was not practical if he intended to spend much time with the children, because of the distance and the limited space. He admitted his primary motivation was "getting out." He agreed that he needed to reconsider having enough bedrooms for the children to spend nights with him and to be in a location for easier access to their friends, school, and other activities. They agreed that they would wait two weeks before telling the children of their decision. During this period they would plan the details of their separation and Jim would find a more convenient apartment.

Through the next two sessions Janet expressed more of her anger about Jim wanting to leave and having a girlfriend. Jim shared some of his guilt. Janet was doing somewhat better with her growing depression. They worked out a time to tell the children together, a time when Jim would take the children to see his new apartment before the move, and a plan to begin dividing up some of their personal and household belongings.

The children heard their discussion about separation and divorce with mixed responses. Michael tried to act cool and put up a good front. He told his father angrily that he was glad he was leaving, that they didn't need him around anyway. He said that he'd take care of the family and that his father never cared about them anyway. He said it wouldn't be that different since his dad was gone all the time anyway.

Donna began to cry as soon as the divorce message became clear to her. She told them they couldn't do this to her, that it wasn't fair, that she hated them. She asked what was going to happen to them. She admitted that she was scared of Dad not being there at night. Her fear and sadness were heartbreaking. She cried for hours that night, and Janet held her like a baby until she fell asleep.

Andy, the fidgety little imp of the family, was uncharacteristically quiet and subdued as the parents explained their feelings and intentions. He seemed almost relieved that all of his earlier confusion was finally explained. He took in some of what they were saying but his big brother's anger and his sister's sadness were very frightening. A lot of what his parents said was lost in his confusion and fear. All he knew was that it began to feel like the end of the world and he didn't quite know how to feel or act. So he sat dry-eyed, quiet, and afraid, wishing he was older and stronger and that he understood better.

Two weeks into the separation Janet was experiencing a mixture of loneliness and anger that was beginning to cause more depression. Jim was enjoying the physical space but struggling with missing the children and his guilt about Janet's pain. He was finding that all this was disrupting his relationship with Linda much more than he imagined. One rainy Saturday night, he had just returned home from dropping off the children when he received a call from Janet.

She was crying and asked him to come back over because she needed him to be there. At first he reminded her that they shouldn't do anything to confuse the children. She said they were asleep and that he could sneak in through their bedroom window, which she would leave open. To Jim she sounded sad and yet somewhat seductive. As he would describe later, there was an element of adventure and danger involved that night.

In any case he went back, they fell into each other's arms, and reportedly made love all night. Janet said later that she couldn't remember him having ever been so loving and passionate, even early in their marriage. He was there in the morning when the children woke up. They thought it was a magical dream come true to find their dad in bed with their mom that morning.

They spent that day and night together, despite our warnings about how that could seriously confuse and anger the children if it was only temporary. Jim left early Monday morning to return to his apartment to change for work. Janet assumed that he would be back that night, but he didn't come, didn't even call.

Jim was an emotional mess that day. He said he felt drawn to go back home to the family but also knew inside that he really had no love left for Janet. He was amazed at how passionate their lovemaking had been, but gradually explained it to himself as dangerous and doing something he knew he shouldn't. The experience did help him distance somewhat from his relationship with Linda and had the effect of making him feel sure that he needed to be on his own.

These events represented Jim's movement through stage 5 (Pseudoreconciliation), where he was having second thoughts about the divorce, and where loneliness and guilt led him back to Janet's bed. Following this experience he remembered the things we had said about second thoughts and the seductive feeling of security about returning home. He said understanding this helped him rethink his relationship with Linda and begin to prepare himself for the divorce (stage 6, Pre-divorce Fantasies).

When Janet learned of this she became enraged, feeling deceived and sexually exploited. She rushed out to see her attorney the next afternoon. Feeling angry and now vindictive, she told her attorney to "file for sole custody and get everything out of this jerk that you can." Unfortunately, by the time Janet and Jim returned for their next session we had a real mess on our hands. In fact Janet came only at the urging of Sandy and her attorney.

It was a tough hour. Jim was apologetic and defensive, Janet was in a rage. We helped them talk through the prior Saturday and Sunday nights. We reminded them of the feelings we had discussed several weeks earlier, feelings that would inevitably occur during a separation. Finally they resolved to move on and asked us to mediate as much of their divorce as possible. Janet was still hurt inside, but this experience helped her distance more from the relationship and she never again pleaded for reconciliation. In fact, she became much more cautious and distrustful of Jim, even in the mediation process.

Both had entered stage 7, the Decision to Divorce, and the dance was indeed over. They came very close to being pushed into an adversarial divorce. If Janet's attorney had not been patient and conciliatory and encouraged her back to that joint session, they could easily have become locked into a way of custody and revenge. Over the next five sessions we helped them put together the Model Mediated Divorce Agreement (stage 9) that appears in Appendix C. Now that you know more about their story, read through their agreement to see how it was translated into a custody and access plan and how they divided their assets and debts.

We expect that if they had pursued the adversarial divorce (stage 10), Janet could have gained sole custody. The basis for this would not have been Jim's affair, since that would not have been entertained in the no-fault procedures of Arizona. However, Janet had been the primary caretaker for the children for most of their early years. While Jim felt close to them, he had been away a lot, building his business. Many judges still favor the role of a mother as the primary custodial parent and Jim probably could not have won a court fight over this. If this had gone to court, the division of property and assets, on the other hand, would have probably looked very much like that which appears in the agreement. They did not have too much to fight over and there are only so many ways to divide these sorts of things.

While the attorneys were reviewing their final agreement, Jim came in to talk to Craig. He was having some second thoughts again (stage 8, Recurring Ambivalence). He had found the entire process draining. Even though he was happy with the results of the mediated agreement, he found himself remembering that weekend a couple of months earlier that he and Janet spent together. He was still puzzled and surprised by his attraction and sexual energy toward Janet. During the past month he had been more preoccupied at work and he had found his relationship with Linda beginning to cool.

Jim struggled quietly with these thoughts for several weeks and finally recognized for himself that he didn't really need the relationship with Linda as badly as he had felt in the early part of the separation and divorce. He was able to recognize that she had compensated for his marital unhappiness and he no longer needed to hang on to her or Janet. He felt more able to begin to go on with his life now as a single father and adult.

Janet and Jim did pretty well during the first year following the divorce. They came in to see us a couple of times for some concerns about their access schedule and some adjustment issues with Donna. Michael wanted to spend a little more separate time with his dad, so we helped them restructure their access plan. Janet went through a few months where she felt that Jim was being too casual in discipline with the kids. She fussed at him for not paying more attention to their homework when they were with him. He became angry at her suggestions that he was not a good father and complained about how much she was gone and the men she was dating (stage 11, Co-Parenting After the Divorce).

One weekend when Michael was with his father, he announced, "Mom is going to marry Robert next month." Jim was astounded that this would come from his son and not from Janet (stage 12, When One Parent Decides to Remarry). He overreacted and rushed over to her house to confront her in front of the other children. Janet was angered by his intrusion but somewhat apologetic about not telling him. She acknowledged later that she had a gut sense that Jim might not accept her remarriage very well. He and Linda had broken up about six months earlier and he had not been active socially. Unfortunately, Jim began to quiz the children about Robert every time they were with him. Soon Donna and Andy began to tell their mother that they did not want to visit their father as often. This shocked Jim, and he and Janet agreed to come in for a joint session.

Jim explained that he had been more lonely than he had expected and the timing of Janet's marriage was bad. He had even been having fantasies of getting back together with Janet. He recognized the problem of quizzing the children and agreed that now that he and Janet had talked about this he could handle it better.

Two months after Janet's marriage to Robert, Jim became frustrated with the children and their continual talk of "how much fun Robert is" and "how happy Mom is now." He became angry at the children and told them he did not want to hear about their mother and Robert any more.

In addition, the children were telling him that their grandparents (Janet's parents) wanted them to come visit them more often and had said; "You don't need to spend so much time with your father. He doesn't do anything with you and also he's the one who made you and your mother so unhappy."

Needless to say, Jim was both hurt and angered by this. He had felt that these in-laws had always liked him and had respected them for trying to stay out of the divorce process. Now he was surprised there was so much resentment toward him and that they were openly sharing it with the children. We recommended that he talk this over with Janet, and although at first she denied that her parents were doing this, she later asked them to leave these issues alone.

Jim found himself feeling pressure to remarry. Often the kids would let him know how they would like him to find someone. They would often point out likely women while walking in the mall. Once Andy had asked his recently divorced teacher if she would like to go out with his father. Fortunately, Jim took his time. It was about a year later that he discussed with the children that he was thinking about marrying Susan (stage 13, the Second Remarriage). They had known her for about six months and seemed happy with their dad's decision.

Donna, who was now almost thirteen, was the one reluctant child. Susan had been married before and had two young daughters aged eight and six. The more time they all spent together, the more Donna felt left out. She was hurt when she saw her dad laughing and playing with Susan's little girls. For a while she tried to cling to her father whenever the two children were present. Soon she just decided to stay home with her mother more often. The children did not have this adjustment problem when their mom married Robert because even though he had been married before he had no children.

We conducted a family session with Jim and Susan and Jim's three children about two months after they had been married (stage 14, Forming a Blended Family). This helped Jim and Susan define their new parenting roles with the children and it gave the children, particularly Donna, an opportunity to express their feelings about Susan's two daughters. Susan and Jim handled this well and asked for some help in redefining their access plan with Janet and Robert so it was coordinated with the times Susan's daughters were with their biological father.

At the time of this session, it was going on three years since the divorce. While Janet and Jim had experienced several stuck places, they had both gone on with their lives. It seemed that both of them and their children had made a healthy adjustment to the family's divorce.

Michael held on to some of his anger about the divorce, which created some difficulties for him as he began to date. He was often impatient and distant with his dates. As he matured he slowly recognized both parents' contributions to the breakup, and he was able to form close bonds with both his mother and his father, although he remained fairly cautious with both of his new stepparents.

Donna blossomed as she entered high school. She became very popular and quite active. Gradually her dependency on her parents decreased and she was able to divide her time more comfortably between the two households. When she was sixteen she asked to spend more time at her mother's home, and Janet and Jim agreed to this change. She wanted simply a more consistent home base and felt somewhat closer to her mother now than her father. (It's common for adolescents to want more time with their same-sex parent). In some ways she was also avoiding the presence of Susan's daughters.

Andy grew taller and seemed comfortable in both parents' homes. He made good friends with Susan's two daughters and was able to maintain strong ties to both parents. He thoroughly enjoyed his access plan, which was now alternating weeks in each home.

We hope this glimpse of Janet and Jim and their family's divorce experience helps illustrate the fourteen stages that we have discussed in this book and shows you ways to make your own divorce experience a healthy one.

Good luck!

# 11

## Questions and Answers About Healthy Divorce

O VER THE MANY YEARS that we've been counseling couples and families about healthy divorce, some important questions have come up time and time again. Here are some of the questions we hear most often from both parents and children.

### PARENTS' TEN MOST FREQUENTLY ASKED QUESTIONS

**1. How can I be sure that getting a divorce is the right thing to do?**
Rarely is anyone 100 percent sure about the decision to divorce. There is often some remaining ambivalence, however small. The questions may linger for years. But you know it's the right thing to do when you become convinced that there is no hope of the marriage returning to a mutually satisfying state. Many people will say that they "knew in my guts" that it was truly over.

Sometimes, a brief meeting with the spouse after being separated awhile confirms the rightness of the decision. It helps you realize that even though you are separated, the old, destructive patterns persist.

You may not be truly sure for a year or more after the divorce—when the adjustment period is past and you suddenly realize one day that you are finally happy again.

### 2. Do you think a separation will help save our marriage or make it worse?

Separations, if carefully planned and mutually agreed to, can be very useful, especially in relationships that have become highly conflicted or volatile. The separation can allow for some new objectivity and time for reflection. It will give you and your spouse some temporary distance that can allow the conflicts to settle down. A separation can also give you a chance to try on a new lifestyle and see how it fits.

Research suggests that separations lasting longer than nine months have lower rates of success for reconciliation. Separations should be time limited and expectations and interactions should be clearly defined. The optimal separation would include both spouses working together with a family therapist to learn as much as possible from the experience.

### 3. Should we stay together until the divorce is final?

Staying together after deciding to separate or divorce can be painful and potentially destructive for everyone—spouses, children, and extended families. It's just simply not reasonable to expect that you can live under the same roof and try to keep the family intact, even if you and your spouse are sleeping in separate bedrooms. It doesn't work! Spouses are hurt, angry, and sensitive, which leads to more reactivity; children get pulled into the conflict; and eventually attorneys and the legal process can make this situation unbearable.

You need to work out a separation plan soon after the decision is made. Get the help of a family therapist or mediator if possible. In some states it may be advisable to have an attorney prepare a legal separation and at least define issues of the children's residence, access, and financial responsibilities in a temporary document that would be in effect during the separation.

If finances prevent an immediate separation, the best you can do is try to lead separate lives. Come and go at different times, sleep in different bedrooms, eat separately, try to divide up activity time with the children, try to be as neutral and respectful of each other as possible. Go out of your way to keep the children out of this experience, since it can have damaging results for them.

## 4. When should we tell our children about our decision to get a divorce?

Don't rush into this, and don't do it impulsively. Always try to tell them together. Don't try to get a one-up position with the kids by trying to be the one to tell them first. As soon as you have both agreed that the divorce is going to happen, begin to discuss when and how to tell the children. Normally it's best to wait and tell them after you and your spouse have worked out a general separation and divorce plan. The children may hit you with a lot of questions, and the more specifically you can answer, the more you'll be able to decrease their anxiety.

Remember, however, that children can be surprisingly intuitive; they usually know when serious changes are going on. If their intuitive worries are not acknowledged, their fears can increase even further. So don't put off telling them for too long. They need to know the details of how their everyday lives may be affected. They do not need to hear the emotional details of it all. Be direct, be factual, be brief, and be available to answer their questions and respond to their fears.

## 5. How long will it take before I feel normal again?

People heal from the pain of divorce at very different rates. It depends on many different factors, such as whether you were the one leaving or the one left, whether you are able to rebalance your life financially after the divorce, how adversarial and messy the actual divorce became, and how supportive is your network of family and friends.

The average length of time for adjustment is between one and two years. The time you were separated doesn't really count because that's like being in limbo. Give yourself some time. Don't rush into new relationships. Try to find out why your prior marriage failed. Discover what you need to be happy and "normal" again. If you are struggling with this or it's becoming more and more painful, seek the help of a family therapist or divorce support groups in your community.

### 6. When and how should I introduce my children to my new boyfriend or girlfriend?

There is no particular need for the children to be part of early casual dating after the divorce. A simple introduction should suffice: "This is my friend Bill; we're going to the movies tonight." Let the children know in a casual way that you are going to begin more social activities.

As a more significant relationship develops, the children should be gradually introduced to this person and included in certain appropriate but casual activities. Don't try to force a new person into the children's lives, because it can backfire. At first, let the children decide whether to have the new person over or join you in a family activity. This is especially true when you have limited time with your children. They will always resent having to share their precious time with a new companion.

Some fathers who are uncomfortable with single parenting will have difficulty with this. They will tend to rely on their new companion to take over when the children are present. Children will sense this discomfort and feel that the father doesn't really want them around. This in turn can cause them to dislike and resent the new companion, who they'll begin to see as a rival for their father's time. Take your time. Try to always listen to the children's feelings and preferences.

### 7. How can I let the children be with my ex when he or she is with another partner?

New partners and eventually stepparents are inevitable in your lives. You must adjust to these realities without passing on fears or bitterness to your children. As long as your spouse's new companion treats them reasonably and with respect, you must allow your children to develop their own feelings and relationships with this new person in their life. If you try to force them to align with you against their other parent's new partner, it can create serious scars for them and potentially backfire in the future.

If this situation is causing you serious pain and resentment, it's probably more your issue than the children's. Consult a family therapist to help you get past these feelings. You need to allow and encourage your children to love all the adults in their lives freely and openly.

If they complain to you about the new partner—and they probably will, if only to let you know they're still loyal to you—tell them that their feelings are important but that they need to share them directly with the other parent and new partner. Do not get pulled into the middle of this. Don't react as a rescuer of your children. Do not try to be a go-between or mediator! However, if the complaints actually suggest abuse, then bring this up immediately but privately with your former spouse.

### 8. Will I ever be able to trust anyone again?

Yes you will, but it may take some time. Trust is often lost in the process of divorce. The more difficult and painful the divorce, the greater the loss of trust and the more apprehension about seeking new relationships. Many people go through a period of hating the opposite sex during or after their divorce. Their anger and hurt gets generalized against the entire opposite gender. Discussions with friends or even in divorce support groups can easily turn to the horrible attributes of the opposite sex. Many who have experienced a divorce declare strongly, "I am never getting married again!"

However, as you heal from the divorce and go on with your life, this generalized distrust and bitterness will dissolve. Soon you'll find new partners who can make you happy again and love you in new ways, and your trust will return. If you have been divorced for more than two years and still have these feelings, however, it's time to consult a therapist.

### 9. How can I make sure I won't repeat the same mistakes in a new relationship?

This should be a concern for everyone who has divorced. Statistics show that the divorce rates for second and third marriages are higher than for first marriages. What happens is that people's unique emotional makeup causes them to seek out and be comfortable with the same types of partners. Sometimes this can be very subtle. But the same problem patterns may simply repeat themselves.

Our advice is to work with a family therapist so you can learn about yourself—what you took to the marriage, what role you played in its failure, what you carry with you as a result of the divorce, and what warning flags to watch for in new relationships. This can be one of the most important gifts you can give yourself.

### 10. How can I stop being afraid of being alone?

Our fears have a way of increasing in strength the more we avoid them. The way to stop being afraid is to face this fear. Gradually start defining some alone time for yourself—really alone. Not with the kids there, waiting for the phone to ring; just sit, think, and experience your aloneness. If you were married for many years and did few activities independent of the family, being deliberately alone may be very difficult.

But being alone and being lonely are very different. Aloneness is a resource for being at peace with yourself and in touch with who you are. Loneliness is a condition of being without significant friends or companions. Focus on developing your aloneness. Learn to know yourself again. Explore who you are, grieve if you need to, but enjoy your aliveness. Loss is a great teacher.

Facing fears and overcoming them can become a powerful, strengthening experience. Many people will remember this one battle after divorce as the most significant that they've fought and won. They faced the unknown and found that it held no terrors, only a familiar and loving face—their own!

---

## CHILDREN'S FIVE MOST FREQUENTLY ASKED QUESTIONS

### 1. Why did you stop loving Mommy {or Daddy}?

This question is frequently asked of the parent who is leaving. It has many potential implications. It may mean: "If you can stop loving her, will you also stop loving me?" It can also mean: "How can love just disappear?" or "What did she do wrong that made you not love her any more (so I won't make the same mistake)?" Sometimes it is a plea or manipulation to get you to change your mind and stay in the marriage. So the answer you give is extremely important.

Children need to be told that grownup love is different from the love that parents have for their children, just like the way they love their best friend is different from the way they love their parents. Sometimes grownup love can be lost through years of unhappiness and disagreements. But grownups can still care about the other person without loving them enough to stay married.

On the other hand, children need to understand that parents' love for their children never goes away or changes no matter how angry they may be at each other. Children need a great deal of reassurance that both parents still love them very much, that divorce is between the parents not between the parents and the children. The children need to be told that they can continue to love everyone the way they always have and that the parents' love for them will always be there, even though the parents no longer love each other.

### 2. Will you ever get back together again?

Children need to be told very clearly and without equivocation that Mommy and Daddy will not get back together again. Tell them that you understand that they wish it could be so and that you understand that it would make them happy, but that you tried for a long time and it would only cause more pain and sadness to try again.

Tell them they must accept this decision as final and try to stop wishing and hoping for the two of you to get back together. Tell them that the more they hope for that the more they'll make themselves unhappy. Tell them you are truly sorry but this is one thing you just can't give them.

### 3. Why do you need to be dating people?

Children will resist your dating and socializing because they prefer the familiar patterns in their former family and because they worry that dating will mean being with them less and perhaps loving them less. Older children may also see your dating as ruining all their hopes and wishes for your reconciliation with their other parent.

Therefore, you must tell them that parents need friends their own age to do fun things with just like kids do. Tell them that dating is a way to begin to feel better and be happier, but that no one will ever mean more to you than they do or ever cause you to love them less.

Don't encourage or allow them to be protective of you or evaluate whom you should see, where you go, or how long you should stay out. Try to schedule your social activities when they are with the other parent. This will put them in less direct competition for your time. Answer the questions about the people you are seeing honestly but remember to apply appropriate boundaries. Do not answer inappropriate questions such as "Are you sleeping with him?" "How much money does he make?" or "Has she ever seen you naked?" Simply say, "That is not appropriate for you to be asking."

### 4. Do I have to visit Daddy if he's with that person I don't like?

You need to help your children understand some of the basic aspects of how divorces work legally. They need to know that judges' orders cannot be ignored and the agreements that you and their other parent have made have to be respected. Sometimes this analogy can help: just like you are the parent who is in charge of the rules and consequences in the family, the judge is in charge of the rules that must be followed in society. When a judge orders an access schedule, it is the parents' job to support and enforce that, and serious penalties can result if it isn't done.

If a child doesn't want to visit a parent, it's important to find out why. If the child's reasons do not constitute grounds for returning to court—and they rarely do, since they're usually based on emotional issues—then the child needs to be told something like this: "I understand you don't want to visit Daddy, but I think if you try to talk to him about your feelings that will make you feel better and you'll enjoy being there. It takes time to get used to new people, and you'll probably get to like this new person in time."

Often this question from a child is an attempt to be supportive of a parent who is angry that the other parent is dating. The child thinks you will be glad that she doesn't like this new person either. If this is the case, tell her that it's OK for her to like this person even if you don't, that she can have feelings that are different from yours. Tell her that you want her to like Daddy's new friend because time with her father is very important and you want her to enjoy being there.

This can be very difficult to do, but it is essential that you be positive and encourage children to keep an open mind and not prejudge this new person. Children need to understand that until they are in their teens they do not have the power to choose whether to go or not go for visitation and that you do not have the power to give them permission not to go.

### 5. Why did you break up our family?

Divorces involve complex issues that are often beyond young children's abilities to understand. Typically, children tend to think in black and white terms—good guy or bad guy, right or wrong. Usually both parents have played roles in the causes of a divorce even though one may have made the actual decision to leave.

Children should not be encouraged to blame or find fault. Tell them that you never wanted to break up the family and that you tried hard for a long time not to. But that it was impossible to fix what was wrong with the marriage and that you believed everyone would eventually be a lot happier if Mommy and Daddy started new lives apart from one another

Tell the children that you are still a family. They are a family with Mommy and they are a family with Daddy. Daddy and Mommy just aren't in the same family together any more. Tell them you are truly sorry for all the unhappiness that getting a divorce meant to them, but that you believe it will be lots happier in the future for everyone. Try this analogy: if you break your arm, it hurts some when it gets fixed by the doctor and nothing feels right while the cast is on, but after it mends it's stronger and better than before.

# Suggested Reading List

## BOOKS FOR PARENTS

Bernstein, Anne. *Yours, Mine, and Ours: How Families Change When Remarried Parents Have a Child Together.* New York: Macmillan, 1989.

Blau, Melinda. *Families Apart: Ten Keys to Successful Co-Parenting.* New York: Putnam, 1994.

Burns, Cherie. *Stepmotherhood: How to Survive Without Feeling Frustrated, Left Out or Wicked.* New York: HarperCollins, 1986.

Cohen, Miriam. *Long Distance Parenting: A Guide for Divorced Parents.* New York: New American Library, 1989.

Engel, Marjorie, and Gould, Diana. *The Divorce Decisions Workbook.* New York: McGraw-Hill, 1992.

Fisher, Bruce. *Rebuilding When Your Relationship Ends.* San Luis Obispo, Calif.: Impact, 1992.

Gardner, Richard. *The Parent's Book About Divorce.* New York: Bantam, 1979.

Gold, Lois. *Between Love and Hate: A Guide to Civilized Divorce.* New York, Plenum, 1992.

Mala, Burt. *Stepfamilies Stepping Ahead: An Eight-Step Program for Successful Family Living.* Lincoln, Neb.: Stepfamily Association of America, 1989.

Ricci, Isolina. *Mom's House, Dad's House: Making Shared Custody Work.* New York: Macmillan, 1980.

Savage, Karen, and Adams, Patricia. *The Good Stepmother: A Practical Guide.* New York: Crown, 1988.

Sitarz, Daniel. *Divorce Yourself: The National No-Fault Divorce Kit.* Carbondale, Ill.: Nova, 1991.

Somervill, Charles. *Stepfather: Struggles and Solutions.* Westminster, 1989.

Visher, Emily, and Visher, John. *How to Win as a Step-Family.* New York: Brunner/Mazel, 1991.

Wallerstein, Judith, and Blakeslee, Sandra. *Men, Women, and Children a Decade After Divorce.* New York: Ticknor & Fields, 1989.

Wallerstein, Judith, and Kelly, Joan. *Surviving the Breakup: How Children and Parents Cope with Divorce.* New York: Basic Books, 1980.

## BOOKS FOR CHILDREN

Gardner, Richard. *The Boys' and Girls' Book About Divorce.* New York: Bantam, 1971.

Krasny-Brown, Laurence, and Brown, Marc. *Dinosaurs Divorce: A Guide for Changing Families.* Boston: Little, Brown, 1988.

Richards, Arlene, and Willis, Irene. *How to Get It Together When Your Parents Are Coming Apart.* New York: Bantam, 1976.

Turow, Rita. *Daddy Doesn't Live Here Any More.* New York: Anchor, 1978.

# Organizations That Can Help You Find Professional Resources

Academy of Family Mediators
    1500 South Highway 100
    Golden Valley, Minnesota 55416
    612/525-8670

Call for a list of Academy mediators in your state.

American Association for Marriage and Family Therapy
    1100 17th Street, NW, 10th Floor
    Washington, D.C. 20036
    800/374-2638

Call for referrals to family therapists in your community.

Stepfamily Association of America
    215 Centennial Mall S, Suite 212
    Lincoln, Nebraska 68508
    402/477-STEP

Call for literature, resources, and videotapes helpful to stepfamilies.

Contact the Bar Association in your county or state for referrals to attorneys specializing in divorce or family law.

Contact the Family or Conciliation Court in your community for divorce-related counseling or mediation services.

# Model Mediated Divorce Agreement

## MEMORANDUM OF UNDERSTANDING REGARDING A MEDIATED DISSOLUTION AGREEMENT

*Mother:* Janet Smith

*Father:* Jim Smith

*Children:* Michael, dob 10-12-80

Donna, dob 2-10-83

Andrew, dob 6-15-87

WE, JANET AND JIM SMITH, have entered into this amicable agreement regarding the dissolution of our marriage and the custody of our three children. We believe that we are both capable of providing loving guidance and protection for them and want to continue to share in the responsibilities and privileges of parenthood by providing for their emotional and physical well-being. Therefore, we have agreed to the following:

1. *Custody.* We request that the court award us joint legal and physical custody of three children.

2. *Access.* We agree to an access plan such that all three children will have alternating split weeks with each parent. In week I they will be with their father from Wednesday after school until Saturday

at 12:00 P.M. (noon) and with the mother from Saturday at 12:00 P.M. (noon) until taking them to school on Wednesday morning. This pattern will continue thereafter.

3. *Summers.* We agree that this access plan will continue through the summers except where vacation times are defined. We agree that we may each schedule up to two weeks of vacation time with the boys, and that this may be taken either consecutively or in one-week blocks. We agree to plan and negotiate these vacation periods with at least one month's advance notice. We also understand that this vacation time may be taken at our residences or traveling out of state. In the latter case we agree to provide an itinerary for the other parent and arrange for telephone access at least once a week. We also agree that other special trips may be negotiated for the summer or during the school year.

4. *Holidays.* We agree to share our children's time during major holidays on an equitable basis and in a flexible manner as follows:

| | Mother's year | Father's year |
|---|---|---|
| Christmas Eve/morning to 11:00 A.M. | Even | Odd |
| Christmas Day and overnight | Odd | Even |
| Christmas week | Odd | Even |
| Thanksgiving weekend (Thursday 9:00 A.M. thru Sunday 5:00 P.M.) | Even | Odd |
| Memorial Day weekend | Even | Odd |
| Labor Day weekend | Odd | Even |
| Easter morning (Saturday 7:00 P.M. to Sunday 2:00 P.M.) | Even | Odd |

All other holidays and vacation periods will follow the normal access plan though they may be negotiated in advance for special activities or travel.

5. *Other Special Days.* Our children will spend parental birthdays when requested and Mother's and Father's Days with each respective parent. Their own birthdays will be celebrated with the residential parent on the day of the birthday and at the earliest possible date following the change of residence with the other parent.

6. We agree that our childrens' grandparents and other extended family members are important to their lives and we will encourage and provide them continuing access.

7. For the purposes of joint custody, we agree to consult with each other on substantial issues related to religious upbringing, educational programs or decisions, significant changes in school or social environment, and medical or legal issues which would affect our children in any substantial way. We have discussed religious education and have agreed they will continue in the Presbyterian faith. We have agreed that our children will continue to be enrolled in the Lakeside School District. We agree that they will continue to receive medical and dental care with their current provider. We agree that everyday decisions of a minor nature for our children, including personal hygiene and grooming, will be made by the residential parent. We agree to seek the assistance of a mediator if any unresolvable disputes occur in any of these areas.

8. We agree that should any major life events occur, such as remarriage, geographical relocation, physical or other disabilities, or other unresolvable disputes which would affect the provisions of this agreement, we will seek the assistance of a mediator to define necessary changes.

9. We agree to review the effectiveness of this access and holiday/ vacation plan annually in August of each year. We understand that we are free to negotiate changes but agree that if there are any disputes that we will seek the assistance of a mediator.

10. *Child Support.* Based on the county guidelines the father will pay the mother $800.00 per month for all three children until each child's eighteenth birthday.

11. *Health Insurance*. We agree that the children will continue their coverage on their mother's health and dental plan and that the father will reimburse her on a monthly basis for their full cost. Unreimbursable medical and dental expenses will be the responsibility of each parent based on their precalculated proportions of income (father 60%, mother 40%). Should changes occur in either of our health plans, we agree to negotiate changes to ensure the best coverage for our children.

12. *Personal Property*. We agree that all personal property not identified below has been divided equally prior to the completion of the divorce. The mother will retain the 1988 Toyota and the father will retain the 1986 Jeep.

13. *Division of Debts*. The father will be solely responsible for the payment of his educational loan and personal loan from his aunt. Mr. Smith will assume responsibility for the balances of the Visa, Chevron, and Sears charge cards. Mrs. Smith will assume responsibility for the balances of the Discover card and Foley's account. We agree that there are no other joint debts except the home mortgage.

14. *Division of Assets*. We agree that cash values in checking accounts have been divided equally. The $5,000 savings will be used as credit at the end of this paragraph. IRA accounts of approximately equal value exist in our separate names and will be retained by each of us.

*House*. The house at 5000 Oceanview was valued at $100,000 with an equity of approximately $20,000 and will be deeded to Mrs. Smith. The mortgage and upkeep of the home will become her sole responsibility.

*Business*. The father's accounting business has been appraised independently at $30,000.

*Annuity*. The mother's annuity has been reviewed and it was determined that the father receive a "credit" of $2,500. The father has no annuity.

*Division Summary*. In lieu of the $15,000 representing one half of the value of Mr. Smith's business, Mrs. Smith will receive Mr. Smith's one-half share of the home equity which is $10,000 and his one-half share of the $5,000 savings, which is $2,500. He also has a credit of $2,500 from Mrs. Smith's annuity. This results in an equal value of $15,000 per spouse.

15. *Spousal Maintenance*. The father agrees to pay the mother $300 per month from January 1993 through March 1995 for the purpose of supporting her return to school to complete her teaching degree.

16. *Designation of children for income tax purposes*. The father will claim all three children for income tax purposes. The parents agree to renegotiate this, if necessary, after the mother completes her schooling and is established in her career.

17. *Definition of beneficiaries on life insurance policies*. The mother and father agree to name the three children as co-beneficiaries of his life insurance policy.

We understand that this is not a formal contract but a memorandum of understanding and we wish that the items stated here be incorporated in our final divorce decree.

| | |
|---|---|
| Janet Smith | date |
| Jim Smith | date |
| Craig A. Everett, Ph.D.<br>Mediator | date |
| Sandra S. Volgy, Ph.D.<br>Mediator | date |

# Index

Academy of Family Mediators, 92, 175

Access: children's needs in, 79–84; children's views of, 84–85; children's questions about, 170–171; failures, 83–84; decision-making list for, 72–73; model for, 177–178; planning, 78; and visitation, 77–84 (*See* Divorce adjustment)

Adjustment after divorce (divorce, 99–105

Ambivalence, 5, 18, 25, 28, 68–70

American Association for Marriage and Family Therapy, 175

Anger, 14–15

Attorneys: after mediation, 96; and decision to divorce, 60–61; legal consultation with, 39–40; selection of, 97–99; stuck couples and, 39–40

Blakeslee, S., 77

Blended families, 131–146, 166–167; boundaries of, 140–146, characteristics of, 133; children's manipulations in, 149–151; formation of, 132; subsystems of, 133–140

Children: and access plans, 79–84; adjustment to divorce of, 110–114; alignments with parents, 34; avoiding divorce for, 16; and their awareness of tensions, 27–29; boundaries of, in blended families, 143–146; and dating, 166, 169–170; and fantasies of divorce, 40–41; five most frequent questions by, 168–171; and loyalties to parents, 34; meaning of parental reconciliation to, 55; manipulations

## THE AUTHORS

CRAIG EVERETT received his Ph.D. from the Interdivisional Doctoral Program in Family Studies and Family Therapy at Florida State University. He has directed graduate programs in marital and family therapy and served on the faculties of Florida State and Auburn Universities. He is a past president of the American Association for Marriage and Family Therapy as well as a Fellow and Approved Supervisor for that professional association. He is editor of the *Journal of Divorce and Remarriage* and serves on the editorial boards of six other professional journals. He served formerly as director of the Pima County Conciliation Court. He is currently in private practice and director of the Arizona Institute of Family Therapy in Tucson.

SANDRA VOLGY EVERETT received her Ph.D. in clinical and child psychology from the University of Arizona. She was chief psychologist for the Tucson Child Guidance Clinic and director of Child Advocacy Programs for the Pima County Conciliation Court. She was an adjunct clinical faculty member with the Interdivisional Doctoral Program in Family Studies and Family Therapy at Florida State University and a director of the Southeast Family Institute in Tallahassee. She is currently in private practice and director of clinical education for the Arizona Institute of Family Therapy in Tucson.

The authors have published a number of professional books and articles in the fields of family therapy and divorce.